Energy, Winter, and Schools

Michael W. Kirst, Ed., *State, School, and Politics: Research Directions*

Joel S. Berke, Michael W. Kirst, *Federal Aid to Education: Who Benefits? Who Governs?*

Al J. Smith, Anthony Downs, M. Leanne Lachman, *Achieving Effective Desegregation*

Kern Alexander, K. Forbis Jordan, *Constitutional Reform of School Finance*

George R. LaNoue, Bruce L. R. Smith, *The Politics of School Decentralization*

David J. Kirby, T. Robert Harris, Robert L. Crain, Christine H. Rossell, *Political Strategies in Northern School Desegregation*

Philip K. Piele, John Stuart Hall, *Budgets, Bonds, and Ballots: Voting Behavior in School Financial Elections*

John C. Hogan, *The Schools, the Courts, and the Public Interest*

Jerome T. Murphy, *State Education Agencies and Discretionary Funds: Grease The Squeaky Wheel*

Howard Hamilton, Sylvan Cohen, *Policy-Making by Plebiscite: School Referenda*

Daniel J. Sullivan, *Public Aid to Nonpublic Schools*

James Hottois, Neal A. Milner, *The Sex Education Controversy: A Study of Politics, Education, and Morality*

Lauriston R. King, *The Washington Lobbyists for Higher Education*

Frederick M. Wirt, Ed., *The Polity of the School: New Research in Educational Politics*

Peter J. Cistone, Ed., *Understanding School Boards: Problems and Prospects*

Lawrence E. Gladieux, Thomas R. Wolanin, *Congress and the Colleges: The National Politics of Higher Education*

Dale Mann, *The Politics of Administrative Representation: School Administrators and Local Democracy*

Harrell R. Rodgers, Jr., Charles S. Bullock III, *Coercion to Compliance*

Richard A. Dershimer, *The Federal Government and Educational R&D*

Tyll van Geel, *Authority to Control the School Program*

Andrew Fishel, Janice Pottker, *National Politics and Sex Discrimination in Education*

Chester E. Finn, Jr., *Education and the Presidency*

Frank W. Lutz, Laurence Iannoccone, *Public Participation in Local School Districts*

Paul Goldstein, *Changing the American Schoolbook*

Everett F. Cataldo, Micheal W. Giles, Douglas S. Gatlin, *School Desegregation Policy: Compliance, Avoidance, and the Metropolitan Remedy*

William J. Grimshaw, *Union Rule in the Schools: Big-City Politics in Transformation*

David K. Wiles, *Energy, Winter, and Schools: Crisis and Decision Theory*

Energy, Winter, and Schools

Crisis and Decision Theory

David K. Wiles
State University of New York
at Albany

Lexington Books
D.C Heath and Company
Lexington, Massachusetts
Toronto

Library of Congress Cataloging in Publication Data

Wiles, David K.
    Energy, winter, and schools.

    Includes index.
    1. Decision-making in school management—Case studies. 2. School
buildings—Heating and ventilation—Case studies. 3. School buildings—
Energy consumption—Case studies. 4. Power resources—Case studies.
5. Schedules, School—Case studies. 6. School children—Transportation—
Case studies. I. Title.
LB2819.W54   371.6'2   78-19544
ISBN 0-669-02544-5

Published simultaneously in Canada

Printed in the United States of America

International Standard Book Number: 0-669-02544-5

Library of Congress Catalog Card Number: 78-19544

To Corey and Matthew

Contents

List of Figures

List of Tables

Introduction

The adaptation of a system to alleviate stress caused by some external threat is a process common to all social organizations. When the threat is unique or sufficiently severe the system often adapts in a condition of crisis. These general premises provide guidance for the following story of two city school systems which adapted to the stress of a winter crisis. The processes of educational planning and decision-making which actually occurred in this case reveal some exciting findings for both theory and practice of educational administration. This text presents the details which generated the following conclusions:

1. What constitutes a "winter crisis" may have little to do with the severity of the weather.

2. The rationality of long-range crisis adaptation may not be the same as what is considered rational in short-run crisis adaptation.

3. The type of decision made for adaptation seems related to the combination of perceived threat to existing arrangements and the possibilities of receiving compensatory resources.

4. A description of organizational adaptation which focuses upon the local school center is different from a description of central office activities or the total school system.

5. A description of actual operations associated with organizational adaptation differs from a symbolic interpretation.

6. What constitutes "success" in adaptation seems to differ according to prior decisions both to limit adaptation efforts to certain subsections of the total organization and to carry out the commitment to act "normally" during the crisis.

7. Adaptations made in crisis are not likely to be retained after the threat has passed.

8. A sense of crisis can be generated from both a gradual growth of doubt and a sharp transformation caused by unique challenges.

The following chapters describe and interpret the activities of the Columbus and Cincinnati school systems during winter 1977. We begin with an overview of the study and research format.

1 Overview

Students of organization have long been interested in how decisions are made in times of crisis. Attempts to understand the variations in crisis response have proliferated in the areas of foreign policy and studies of communities caught in natural disasters.[1] Since the 1960s it has become popular for school organizations to undergo a similar type of scrutiny with the hope of understanding crisis response. For example, events of student activism associated with free speech or war protest were documented to determine the type of response from universities. At the public school level, responses to a variety of social crises were studied to find ways to adapt organizations to conditions of human conflict and controversy.[2] An emerging field of study, the politics of education, is, in part, an effort to understand how school organizations retain legitimacy and resources to operate under conditions of competition and challenge.

An essential assumption underlying efforts to understand how schools respond to social crises is that the elements of purposiveness necessary to manage crisis must be identified before adaptation can be meaningful. As the 1970s have progressed, a confidence has grown that the "real" meanings of crisis adaptation are becoming understandable. "Firing line" practitioners and university-based policy analysts seem able to identify the dynamics which underlie coalition formation, or clarify the ingredients of strategy which may determine utility matching.[3] Labels such as "contingency management" and "conflict resolution techniques" give the appearance that schools can respond to crisis and turbulence in a purposive manner.[4]

The growing confidence in having achieved an understanding of purpose, form, and substance of social crisis may have contributed to the essence of this text, for this is a story of how schools responded to a "different type" of crisis condition. It is a story of how school organizations made decisions in response to a crisis that seemed to be neither social nor purposive in terms of a conventional, analytical focus. The "villain" in this study was the winter of 1977 and the unprecedented severe weather which outstripped the limits of what was considered possible needs for natural gas heating fuel. This type of crisis was unique. On the one hand, there was no sudden shift of events such as in an earthquake or tornado. On the other hand, there was no gradual extension of worsening conditions, such as sagging finances or frustrated desegregation efforts. The forces which combined to create the winter of 1977 were to create a novel type of crisis which demanded new patterns of response.

Educators need to understand weather-related crises and the efforts made by Cincinnati and Columbus school officials to adapt to those types of conditions. Whether the particular combination of weather severity and natural gas shortage which occurred in 1977 is replicated exactly in future winters is not too important. Some experts predict an unbroken continuation of harsh winters while others predict a cycle of harsh and mild conditions. What is important about this type of crisis is its total impact on the schooling function. As we will see, this type of crisis cannot be contained as policy issues of facilities or plant operations. Further, a winter-related crisis has both short- and long-term implications for administrative governance and rational planning. The importance of this text rests with its explanation of a type of crisis condition which dramatically affects educational practice and the success of various real-life efforts to adapt to such a crisis condition.

The Problem

From a research perspective, the basic problem was *to describe and explain variation in types of crisis response practiced by school organizations.* The specific study involved the public school systems of Columbus and Cincinnati, Ohio, during winter 1977. Case study analysis provided the basis for inferences concerning environmental and organizational variations in decision response by the two school systems. The specific objectives of case analysis which directed this study were (a) to describe and make inferences about the variation of decision response *within* each school system which could be attributed to winter conditions and (b) to describe and infer comparisons *between* the variations of decision response of the two school systems which could be attributed to winter conditions. Although the phenomena under study precluded the normal methodological requirements of experimentalism[5] the following were considered necessary conditions to conduct an adequate case analysis. To be able to:

1. describe the "normal state" of decision-making prior to and after the winter of 1977;

2. describe the chronology of specific issues which triggered decision responses during winter 1977;

3. describe the adaptive response patterns of each school system during winter 1977.

4. compare the patterns of adaptation between the two school systems during winter 1977.

The basis for inference about variation in crisis response rested with a methodological focus upon six major variables which were used to construct a crude theoretical model of interrelationships.[6] Figure 1-1 schematically illustrates the conceptual scheme for this study.

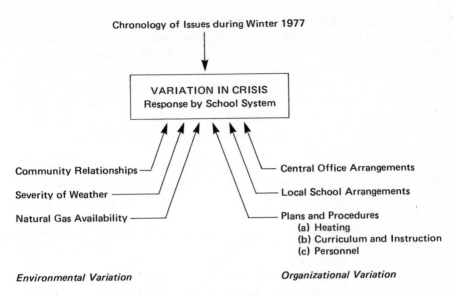

Figure 1-1. Scheme for Case Analysis

It was assumed that the six major variables would adequately identify sources of *inter*organizational and *intra*organizational variations in decision response. While each of the variables in figure 1-1 are explored in detail later, a brief description will be useful now.

Community relationships concerns the roles of the board of education, municipal agencies and local community interest groups and state governmental agencies. The decision to include the board of education as contributing to variations in the environment of the school system was based on the natural boundary between policy system and environment[7] which emerged during this type of crisis condition. As will be noted later, the decision response of this study was essentially a response of the professional educator, with the board acting in a legitimizing role.

Weather severity was considered in terms of actual temperatures, accumulated snowfall, and degree days, which is a statistic used to judge actual heating needs in facilities. Specific impact on schools was also considered as both the demands for minimal building protection and demands to conduct school operations under professionally acceptable conditions.

The final environmental variable which could explain inter- and intraorganizational variations in response was *natural gas availability*. This variable was identified in terms of supply allocated and delivered to the schools, conservation efforts taken prior to winter 1977 to increase supply, conversion of heating units to other than natural gas, and efforts to gain additional emergency supplies of natural gas.

Three other variables were assumed to identify variations of decision response within the school systems. The fourth variable of *existing central office arrangements* was identified by (a) formal organization; (b) role of superintendent of schools; (c) mechanisms responsible for deciding about plant operations and maintenance, for decisions about transportation, for curriculum and instruction decisions, for pupil personnel decisions, and for community service and public relations decisions; (d) the administrative role of coordinating with teacher federation and classified personnel organizations; and (e) the technical role of chief engineer in energy matters.

The fifth variable of *existing local school arrangements* was identified by (a) formal organization, (b) role of principal and other local school administrators, (c) role of teachers, (d) role of janitors, (e) role of parents, and (f) the role of students in a selected sample of local schools.

The sixth variable identified the *existing plans and procedures* which could guide policy decisions concerning heating of school facilities, transportation of pupils, curriculum, instruction, and personnel in times of crisis.

In summary, a crude theoretical model identified six major variables which could explain interorganizational and intraorganizational variations within and between the Columbus and Cincinnati public schools during winter 1977. Each of the six variables under study was identified by specific descriptors used to guide collection of data through case study methodology. Findings which contributed to an understanding of the interorganizational and intraorganizational planning variations provided the grounds for inference about the basic research problem—to describe and explain variation in the type of crisis response practiced by school organizations.

The Case Study

The specific study of school adaptation during winter 1977 represented a special focus within a larger research effort to determine the effect(s) of energy regulation upon schooling practices within Ohio between fall 1976 and spring 1978.[8] A team of fifteen researchers, under the direction of the author,[9] were responsible for fulfilling the special data collection needs during the two months of intensive study which form the core of this study.

Both the Cincinnati and Columbus school systems agreed formally to participate in the specific study of winter 1977 after reviewing a proposal specifying the research objectives, collection format, outcomes of analysis, and use of research results.[10] Direct contact was maintained with the superintendent of schools, appropriate central office staff, and principals of local schools selected for concentrated study. Compilations of raw data and descriptive accounts were given to school officials for their review and comments concerning accuracy and validity. Specific changes noted by practitioners in each system were reviewed and, where appropriate, incorporated into the case study data base.

Data collection involved content analysis of pertinent formal reports, public sources (such as newspapers, media announcements), and informal memoranda. There was considerable reliance upon elite interviews for those key policy actors who occupied key interorganizational and intraorganizational linkages in each school system. Observations and perceptions of key school officials were cross-referenced and verified by critical incident.[11]

Overview

This text is designed to present the reader with a sequentially ordered accumulation of information which leads to practical and theoretical implications about crisis response in school organizations.

Chapter 2 presents chronology of decision events leading up to the winter of 1977, the two months of crisis (January and February), and the aftermath period.

Chapters 3 and 4 discuss the details of environmental variation. Chapter 3 presents the weather severity and the availability of natural gas fuel, and chapter 4 presents the community context of Cincinnati and Columbus.

Chapters 5 and 6 outline the specific details of organizational variation. Chapter 5 describes central office arrangements in the two systems and chapter 6 presents the results of detailed study of a sample of local school centers in each city system. Chapters 7 and 8 describe the plans and procedures used in system-wide and local school decision-making.

Chapters 9 and 10 draw general conclusions about how school organizations respond to the winter type of crisis. Chapter 9 outlines practical implications derived from this study for school officials and boards interested in setting contingency plans for weather-related crisis. Finally, Chapter 10 discusses the theoretical implications of this study for our understanding of decision-making in large organizations and of how systems react to crisis.

Setting the Stage

It seems important to state at the outset that this is a study of two school systems caught unprepared by crisis. It is even more important to note that unpreparedness was not the "fault" of the school officials in charge or due to a cavalier policy attitude toward energy or providing for school services during winter. In fact, just the opposite was true. Columbus and Cincinnati schools both represented jurisdictions with the organizational resources, technical expertise, and professional commitment not to get caught unprepared. The importance of this study is less the documentation of specific events in a particular time frame and more the success and failures of rational planning and administrative decision-making under stressful conditions. In the chronology of events presented in the next chapter we will see that the warnings of an impending crisis were given in several forms. The local schools were more than 70 percent dependent upon a type of fuel that was being curtailed in ever increasing amounts. Many citizens and professionals in 1977 were skeptical that the "energy crisis" was little more than a contrived political maneuver. Finally, neither school system had developed detailed contingency plans to cope with this type of crisis on any mass scale.

In the luxury of hindsight, we may be overly critical of officials in both systems. However, the chronology also documents that the Cincinnati and Columbus schools were given assurances by the public utilities (which supplied the natural gas) that the results of prior planning and conservation guaranteed necessary supplies. The chronology also shows that the winter of 1977 was without precedent in severity and outstripped the response capacity of all governments. Given the "mixed bag" of interpretation, we can appreciate and learn from the real-life experiences of school systems responding to a unique type of crisis.

Notes

1. For example, Graham Allison, *Essence of Decision* (Boston: Little, Brown, 1971), or Allen Barton, *Communities in Disaster* (Garden City, N.Y.: Doubleday and Company, 1969).

2. See, for example, Paul Peterson, *School Politics: Chicago Style* (Chicago: University of Chicago Press, 1976) or Larry Cuban, *Urban School Chiefs Under Fire* (Chicago: University of Chicago Press, 1976).

3. Utility matching is a term from the mathematical gaming literature of decision theory. It means that decision-makers expect that the gains or benefits of winning also contain some costs or loss. Choice then reflects a proportionate balance between winning and losing for all deciders rather than all win or all loss for some players.

4. Understanding of purpose in crisis response does not mean that there is success in adaptation. Obviously school officials still search for the means to deal *successfully* with sagging state finances, "arbitrary" federal regulations, "hostile" publics, and so forth.

5. See rationale of case study methodology in appendix B. For a general discussion of the inapplicability of experimental assumptions for this type of study see Barney Glaser and Anselin Strauss, *The Discovery of Grounded Theory* (Chicago: Aldine Publishing, 1969), or Eugene Haas and Thomas Drabek, *Complex Organizations* (New York: Macmillan, 1973), especially chapter 9.

6. Barton, *Communities in Disaster*, pp. 214-218; Arthur Stinchcombe, *Constructing Social Theories* (New York: Harcourt, Brace and Jovanovich, 1968).

7. Paul Lazarsfeld and Herbert Menzel, "On the Relation between Individual and Collective Properties," in A. Etzioni, ed., *A Sociological Reader on Complex Organizations* (New York: Holt, Rinehart and Winston, 1969), especially pp. 499-516, and W. Richard Scott, "Field Methods in the Study of Organizations," in James March, ed., *Handbook of Organizations* (Chicago: Rand McNally, 1965).

8. With the support of the Department of Educational Leadership, Miami University. A special thanks to Dr. Charles Teckman for his support.

9. This study could not have been accomplished without the voluntary efforts of the following graduate students, administrative staff, and faculty: Carol Barnes, Peggy Bower, Flocka Butt, Alleen Deutsch, Mike Farr, Jan Fulton, Rod Garreton, Charlotte McKensie, Debbie Phillips, Phil Price, Mike Raymond, John Roush, Sally Roush, Paula Saunders, Carol Smith, Ted Wagenaar, and Eldon Wiley.

10. Letters on file. Columbus schools, dated July 1, 1977, and Cincinnati schools, dated July 14, 1977.

11. See appendix B for methodology.

2

The Core of Crisis

The major focus of this study concerns the months of January and February 1977. These were the months when the school systems of Columbus and Cincinnati, Ohio, adapted educational practices to meet the crises of severe weather and the shortage of natural gas heating fuels. The variations of crisis response are vividly portrayed when the Columbus "School Without Schools" attempt to provide new alternative educational services is contrasted with Cincinnati's "host-guest" arrangement, which was designed to replicate normal educative services as much as possible. "School Without Schools" was a system-wide local school reorganization designed by Columbus officials to provide "normal" school one day a week and four days of alternative options. The plan received national acclaim, emphasizing how the detriments of severe weather can be turned into creative and innovative educational opportunities.

The Columbus response to the winter crisis stood in stark contrast to the actions taken by Cincinnati educators. Rather than a massive, radical reorganization of the total school system, Cincinnati adjusted only to the extent necessary to maintain normal operations. The basic research question of this study was to describe and explain the variation in crisis response of the two systems. How and why did Columbus respond one way and Cincinnati the other? What policy factors determined the decision to plan for radical change or the replication of normal operations during the 1977 emergency? The chronology of specific events leading up to the crisis, the events of the crisis itself, and the events of the aftermath help to answer the basic question.

Background

There is no easy way to obtain the background of detail necessary to understand the 1977 context and not risk having the reader become confused by the numerous actors, issues, and intricacies of that time period. In the following discussion concerning the time period 1972 up to January 1977, four major policy events are identified. In addition to the school systems under study, the events identify the major fuel suppliers (Columbia Gas of Ohio and Cincinnati Gas and Electric), the state regulatory agency for fuel (Public Utilities Commision of Ohio), and the state educational interests (State Board and Department of Education). This will help set the stage for later discussions. The reader should not be too concerned with the specific meanings of terms, such as "base allocation" or "large user" schools, which are related to the details of the four major events but will be explained later.

1972 is the first year when any school-related policy body demonstrated interest in issues of energy and weather as educational concerns. Between 1972 and 1975 the major actors concerned with these types of issues were the public utility which serves the Columbus schools (Columbia Gas of Ohio) and the Ohio State Department of Education. Columbia Gas of Ohio was interested to the extent that the utility could gain a gas curtailment plan which would affect the public schools. In July 1972 Columbia Gas of Ohio filed such a plan with the state public utilities commission (responsible for regulating energy supply and use) and established winter and summer seasons for determining how much natural gas fuel a particular customer was to be allocated.[1] Until 1972 the concept of base allocation of a limited amount of fuel was not specified. After the 1972 plan was recognized by the public utilities commission (hereafter P.U.C.O., for Public Utilities Commission of Ohio) schools were allocated a specific amount for a designated winter season and another amount for the summer season.

Although it was not recognized in 1972, the Columbia Gas of Ohio plan was to have two major effects upon the circumstances of winter 1977. The plan was later to provide a basis for differential curtailments of base allocations (for example, cut the Columbus school winter allocation 40 percent and the summer allocation 15 percent) and, more important, structure emergency planning efforts. During winter 1977 much of the school planning was based upon how to reach the end of the winter allocation season rather than calculating actual cold weather and heating need constraints.

In October 1975 the base allocation season plan was modified to spell out specific curtailment levels for natural gas customers.[2] A second event which was to have considerable impact in winter 1977 was yet another modification of the original season plan made in May 1976. After judging the results of user conservation efforts made during winter 1975 as a result of actual curtailments being imposed, P.U.C.O. made a ruling which rewarded energy-conscious customers. An exemption to winter season curtailments was given to natural gas customers who lowered consumption below a certain amount through permanent conservation measures. Although intended to be an inducement for conservation, the spring 1976 P.U.C.O. ruling had another policy effect. Columbus and Cincinnati school officials became convinced that their conservation efforts (at that time Columbus had been under some curtailments for two winters and Cincinnati for one winter) had made extreme heating fuel shortage a moot issue. Because both school systems had lowered actual consumption below their curtailed base allocations they assumed they were now exempt from further limitations upon natural gas supplies.[3]

A third major precrisis event occurred on the last day of 1976. On this date, P.U.C.O. allowed the public utility serving the Columbus schools to raise actual curtailment of base allocations 10 percent. The impact of this judgment was a formal recognition that past impressions about fuel availability and planning based upon conservation were illusions. The coldest November on record had caused Columbus schools and other natural gas customers to overconsume their monthly allocation and "borrow" in hopes that December 1976 would be mild enough to compensate.[4] By the end of December the state regulatory commission reluctantly agreed[5] with natural gas suppliers that the existing curtailments were not enough. The impact of the 10 percent rise in curtailment was "the straw that broke the back" of the Columbus schools and ultimately shifted the thinking of planners from compensations to maintain normal conditions to wholesale reorganization for an unprecedented emergency.

A fourth precrisis event, somewhat related to the critical decisions involving natural gas regulators, suppliers, and users, was the continuing role of the Ohio State Department of Education to make energy availability an educational issue. As early as October 1973 the State Department of Education (hereafter SDE) appointed an energy coordinator. On November 11, 1974, the Ohio State Board of Education formally declared the availability of sufficient energy to operate schools to be "a problem of major dimensions." The basic argument of the board's resolution was that closing schools for 2.6 million Ohio children would be counterproductive to fuel conservation as "heating, cooking, recreational, and transportation needs are less in central facilities than in individual homes. . . . [In central facilities] body heat is generated to maintain room temperature comfort."[6] The resolution indicated that formal state actions by educational agencies would be confined to providing "technical assistance" to local districts and calling "special attention" to the plight of the schools. Neither of these early declarations of action would have true influence on the intricate policy dynamics of natural gas fuel scarcities during the real crisis. However, the actions of the SDE and State Board of Education in recognizing crisis potential were important.

In summary, four major events of the precrisis period from 1972 until the winter of 1977 set the stage for the crisis. The major events were to have significant impact on the 1977 crisis, although no one could foretell the impact at the time of the particular event. First, the P.U.C.O. ruling of 1972 was important in making the concept of natural gas curtailments a way of policy life for fuel consumers. The establishment of seasons with differential curtailment levels affected later school system planning to survive the heating season of winter 1977.

The May 1976 P.U.C.O. *Report* was important in creating the illusion that systematic conservation efforts taken by the schools and other customers had alleviated the crisis nature of a natural gas fuel shortage. School officials knew that the days of "short supply" would remain but the ability to meet previously imposed curtailments (40 percent of large school users in Columbus, 20 percent in Cincinnati) seemed to indicate that the winter heating of schools would remain manageable.

The third major event of the precrisis, occurring at the end of December 1976, signaled the end to the illusion that the winter of 1977 was to be a "manageable operation" based upon prior planning efforts. The ability of the public utility to raise gas curtailments to 50 percent negated the total conservation effort and last hopes that the schools could sustain normal heating "at the margin."

The final important event was the continuing efforts of the State Board and State Department of Education to establish energy use and fuel shortage as educational issues. As will become apparent, the public schools of Ohio were in fierce competition with other natural gas customers for available supplies. The classification of the public schools as a particular type of "domestic" user made the crucial differences of "if and when" curtailments would be imposed by a public utility. The State Board and SDE waged a vigorous campaign to have schools be assured of heating fuel supplies. The 1974 board statement initiated a three-year attempt to exempt schools from curtailment of their base allocations of natural gas.

With this background, we now turn to the specific events of the two-month period between January and February 1977, which was the core of crisis.

The Cincinnati Crisis

The true nature of the winter crisis began in January 1977. During the normal twenty school days that month, the Cincinnati schools were completely closed eight days. In addition, the conventional meaning of schooling was altered another nine days in January due to curtailment or serious disruption of transportation services. A major policy characteristic of the Cincinnati school system was that 29,000 pupils (approximately one-fourth of all pupils) relied on metropolitan bus service, contracted yellow bus, or independent taxis to attend local schools. During January metro transportation, which handled the majority of students, was curtailed three days while taxis and contracted buses were curtailed an additional six days. Thus there were several January days when Cincinnati schools were, on paper, operating normally with somewhat less than 40 percent of the total student population in actual attendance.[7]

During February, fifteen of the largest schools (one-eighth of the total pupil population) were closed and the students attended alternative facilities under a "host-guest" arrangement. On the other hand, there was no disruption in any of the pupil transportation services during the entire month.

Cincinnati schools purposively avoided taking advantage of the fifteen reimbursable "energy emergency days" made possible (on February 2) by the state legislature. The superintendent of schools announced an anticipated extra cost of $100,000 to keep the schools open during January and February but stipulated that the district's goal was to "say we have closed schools fewer days than any district in the state of Ohio."[8]

January Events

When the schools were notified in early winter 1977 that the large natural gas user schools were to be curtailed 20 percent of the base allocation by the new year, Cincinnati school officials assumed that existing conservation measures were adequate to meet possible shortages. During the previous winter (1976), Cincinnati schools had reduced gas consumption 19 percent from their base allocation.[9] With notification of a mandatory 20 percent curtailment of base allocation in January 1977, school officials implemented long-standing plans to close one school and to convert two large user schools to coal and another two facilities to oil. At the time, the effect of continued conservation and fuel conversion seemed more than adequate to meet Cincinnati Gas and Electric's mandate for reduced consumption. The major energy problem of mid-January 1977 seemed less how to keep the schools warm than how to get the children to the buildings. After a two-day attempt to open after the New Year's holidays the schools closed for a day because of inclement weather. The following two days, the contracted private buses (hereafter yellow) and taxis refused to provide transportation on grounds that insurance coverage would be void.

The second school week in January found the system closed completely on Monday (the tenth) and no pupil transportation (metro or private) on Tuesday and Wednesday. Although metro transportation was partially restored on Thursday and Friday (January 13 and 14) the normal school arrangement was still disrupted.

It was the at the end of the third week that the Cincinnati central office conceded that normal routines and organization could not cope with this severe a crisis. Plans were initiated to run the entire school system on a day-to-day basis *vis-à-vis* assessment of inclement weather conditions.

Whether the day-to-day planning model could have worked became academic when, on Friday, January 28, 1977, Cincinnati Gas and Electric curtailed natural gas to 80 percent of the large user schools. Further, CG and E requested a voluntary 30 percent curtailment of all forty-eight small gas user schools in the district. The effect of this dramatic curtailment was swift; all Cincinnati schools closed.

The Peak of Crisis

The time frame from Thursday, January 27, through Monday, January 31, represents the fundamental decision period for school adaptation to extreme crisis. In less than a month the school system had been transformed from an organization relying upon normal operations and standard procedures to one reacting on a day-to-day basis, to one being closed completely by winter crisis. For a short time during the peak of the crisis, the essential governance of the schools shifted beyond reliance on temporary committees and contingency plans for emergencies to the judgments of three key individuals. The individuals were specialists in the areas of transportation, plant maintenance, and school administration activities which involved coordination among local schools. None of the three was at the assistant superintendent or above level of administration, although each worked closely with a superior who held such a rank. The three persons spearheaded emergency decisions to reestablish transportation, facilities heating, and alternative local school organizational arrangements for the upcoming month of February. Based upon the emergency efforts taken during the peak of crisis, the following policy options were generated:

Alternative 1: Close all schools through Friday, February 4.

Alternative 2: Open all schools except the fifteen large users starting Tuesday, February 1.

Alternative 3: Open all schools except the fifteen large users on Tuesday and *reschedule* the students in these schools to other schools starting on Wednesday, February 2.

Alternative 4: Open all nongas schools on Tuesday. Close *all* gas schools through Friday.

Alternative 5: Open all nongas schools on Tuesday. Reschedule all gas school students into nongas schools beginning Thursday, February 3.

Alternative 6: (Recommended) Open all nongas schools on Tuesday. Close all gas schools on Tuesday while teachers prepare homework assignments. Open all gas schools (including the fifteen large users) on Wednesday, at which time teachers will give assignments for the rest of the week. Wednesday would be an abbreviated schedule, perhaps two hours or less.

Alternate Plans for Week of February 6, 1977

Plan A: If only the fifteen high user gas schools continue to be closed, reschedule them in existing nongas schools (this rescheduling plan is completed, but must be communicated to the staff).

Plan B: If *all* gas schools continue to be curtailed, schedule all of them in nongas schools. This plan has not been developed and we are not sure of its feasibility. Certainly much double scheduling of schools, especially junior highs, will be necessary. This rescheduling plan probably should not be reported by the media at this time as it would tend to confuse the already complicated communication necessary. If we do implement it (decision by Friday, February 4) we will need media support to do it.[10]

A rough interpretation of the generated options would be, if we can limp through the first week of February with minimum strain on transportation and plant heating then a detailed plan to get local schools operating on a sustained basis can be implemented the second week (week of February 6).

Assessment of plant heating, transportation capacity, and reorganization options indicated *Alternative 6* and *Plan A* as most feasible. *Plan A* became known as the host-guest pairing plan. This plan was implemented throughout the rest of February, and the rescheduling of 11,000 pupils in large user gas schools to nongas schools affected nearly one-eighth of the children in the district.

In general, regular students in elementary schools (the hosts) attended class from 8:00 a.m. to noon. Students from the closed school (the guests) attended the site from 1:00 to 5:00 p.m. Secondary-school hosts also held classes from 8:00 a.m. until noon, and classes for the guests from 2:00 to 6:00 p.m.

Metro buses ran routes for students of closed schools and took them home at their regular dismissal times. The eighty-five other schools in the Cincinnati system ran normal schedules throughout the crisis month of February. Although normal schedules were maintained, energy-associated conditions were not. For the forty-two natural gas small user schools, the thermostats were set at 60°. Thermostats at another thirty-eight nongas schools were reduced to 65°. At night, thermostats in all schools were set at 35-40°.

February Events

The host-guest pairing began on Wednesday, February 3, with the novelty of a new situation making most curricular and instructional adjustments manageable. The newspapers were filled with local-color stories of the student excitement at novelty. However, a crack in the rosy picture soon developed; the split schedule transportation plan originally envisioned was proving to be unfeasible. The daily, on-off judgment on whether to conduct school during the peak of the crisis had precluded establishing normal schedules of route transportation. More significant, a later modification of the initial pairing plan implemented during the first week in February increased the involvement to twenty-five schools and approximately 20,000 pupils requiring bus transportation. This load required a minimum of 150 buses to operate two shifts, and there were only 80 buses to be contracted in the entire city.[11]

Finally, on February 8, 1977, the growing pupil transportation crisis was resolved. The adjustment involved metro picking up five canceled contracted bus routes, with the pupils involved being issued extra metro tokens. In addition, twenty extra contracted buses were established on a three-split schedule and twenty extra taxi trips per day were financed.[12] The approximate additional cost per day was $1,900, and the estimate to continue this service throughout February was $21,750.[13]

There was a second part to the transportation problem which became apparent as soon as the pairing plan was implemented. On February 7, 1977, the Metropolitan Area Religious Coalition of Cincinnati protested that neither the children in the host schools nor those in the guest schools were receiving school lunches.[14] A week later, the superintendent explained to the Board of Education that the issue was being handled "on a school by school basis" and that the possibility of "box lunches that could be eaten on the buses is being explored." The nature of the problem revolved around the split transportation schedule and modified curriculum scheduling (that is, secondary students were in thirty-five-minute class periods) which caused the normal times for eating lunch to conflict with the bus service and/or instructional activities. On February 16, 1977, students were provided box lunches to eat on their way to or from the paired schools.

This, then, represented the core of the Cincinnati crisis response to winter 1977: a transportation modification involving one-fourth of the public, and a local school reorganization involving one-eighth of the pupils in the district. Throughout the February ordeal the main policy theme was to approximate normal conditions whenever possible. By the middle of the fourth week of February, "the crisis" was, in effect, over. Average temperatures were in the high forties, and no snow remained on the ground. CG and E removed all curtailment to base allocation on March 1, 1977. On March 2 all thermostats were raised to 65°; all pupils returned to normal, precrisis schedules; and the special bus token plan was discontinued.

The only other major policy implication related to the February crisis response also involved transportation. First, the SDE refused to pay additional reimbursement for emergency modifications (for example, double and triple shifts of students not normally transported) to the transportation formula. Second, desegregationists attempted to argue that emergency adjustments for energy reasons demonstrated that busing to achieve racial desegregation was feasible. The latter issue could have had important policy implications in that busing per se had been a crucial point of dispute in a long-standing court battle between Cincinnati schools and the NAACP. However, the school system argued through the newspapers that the school pairings were based upon geography, size, and fuel used and, therefore, involved transfer of children of predominantly the same race. While this argument seemed implicitly to argue an existing segregated school system, the busing aspect lost its political visibility over time.

We now turn to the story of how the Columbus school system adapted to the months of January and February 1977.

The Columbus Crisis

During January 1977 Columbus schools were closed five regular school days. During February, under the instructional program labeled "School Without Schools," normal school operations were curtailed fifteen days (although only twelve were counted as "energy days" because of an agreement with the State Department of Education).

January Events

The new year began with Columbia Gas of Ohio announcing that the agreed-upon curtailment of 40 percent (for large gas users) was being raised to 50 percent. Although the raise in curtailment level was significant in terms of fuel availability, the real impact upon policy planning was the recognition that past conservation success was not related to who got curtailed. The last hopes of the schools being spared or exempt from curtailment were dashed.

On January 3, the Energy Crisis Committee[15] outlined the condition of the Columbus Public Schools and possible options for emergency adaptation. Among the points made was the first hint of a local school organizational arrangement which would become "School Without Schools."[16]

It was clear from the start that the Columbus Public Schools would *not* approach the strategy of energy crisis adaptation with an internal focus. The formulation of a "self-help" gas task force on January 10, 1977, was an immediate response by the schools as it became increasingly clear that Columbia Gas of Ohio could not provide emergency gas needs by existing arrangements. The schools initiated attempts to secure alternative sources through a nonprofit group called Gas, Inc.[17]

Six days later, January 16, the Columbus schools were notified informally that natural gas allotments were to be curtailed 85 percent. This meant, effectively, that the Columbus schools would not operate.

Thus, by mid-January, the policy postion of the Columbus schools boiled down to one of being "out of business" if state-wide rules and regulations that defined Ohio public education were not modified. On January 19, 1977, the following informal position paper was circulated by the Columbus Superintendent of Schools to key members of the state legislature, governor's office, and State Department of Education:

> With the latest Columbia Gas curtailment of 85%, the Columbus Schools have only enough gas to last until February 17. The gas allocation would then be totally gone. In order to avoid the prohibitively expensive process of mothballing schools, the schools should be closed now, and we would need to remain closed until April 3 when the new allocation begins.
>
> In short, we face a crisis of monumental proportions. Relying solely on voluntary measures at this stage is unrealistic. Permitting various school districts to do "their own thing" will create even more problems. We need a state-wide plan with legislative requirements.
>
> Listed below are suggestions that ought to be part of whatever plan is adopted:
>
> 1. The current calendar requirement of 182 days should be modified.

A number of emergency days should be designated. Legislation should be enacted that would make it unnecessary to make up at least one half of the days lost because of the energy crisis.

2. If schools are closed, we face substantial unemployment compensation payments that would be an added expense. Some relief should be provided either through state reimbursement to school districts or enabling districts to pay personnel for all or a portion of the energy days.

3. Consideration should be given to developing alternative educational efforts while schools are closed, such as radio, television, newspaper lessons, plus home tutoring, home visits, telephone tutoring, or special centers established in the recreation centers, churches, or buildings that have available fuel. This is complex and frought with problems, but if school personnel are paid for days schools are closed, they should be available to provide service to the students on whatever basis is feasible.

4. Schools should not be mothballed. The problems of draining the water, cutting pipes, putting antifreeze in traps, etc., are more substantial than most people realize.

5. All holidays and school recesses that were scheduled in the calendar during the remaining days in the school year should be rescheduled as a part of the time school is closed during the energy emergency.

6. Provisions to make up days lost should be flexible. Adding an hour per day to the school calendar should be permitted, with one day of credit counted for each additional five hours completed as one possible way of making up days lost.

The extent of success in influencing alteration of state-wide constraints on energy crisis adaptation can be inferred in the later rationales of Governor James Rhodes when declaring a state-wide natural gas emergency, in the legislature passage of emergency compensation bills (SB51 and HB176), and in SDE interpretations of what constituted energy emergency days. In short, the Columbus public schools became the visible example of school adaptation effort being undertaken in the entire state.

As could be expected, internal strategies for crisis adaptation were coordinated to expected changes in the conventional statewide meanings of public education. By the twenty-first day of January, central office administrators began working upon the details and documents necessary to conduct a massive local school reorganization plan called "School Without Schools." It was clear that normal schooling was becoming an increasingly difficult task.[18] Further, it was shown that, as of February 4, the Columbus schools would face a deficit of natural gas amounting to *166.4 million* cubic feet needed to finish the April 3 deadline for the heating season.[19] In mid-January the real issue became *how* the schools would modify normal education conditions, not *if* they would change. All internal efforts shifted to "School Without Schools" planning.

The Peak of Crisis and "School Without Schools"

"School Without Schools" was what Fred Hechinger described as an "unorthodox remedy...where the emergency forced the bureaucracy to say 'yes' rather
than 'no' to unorthodox ideas and requests...and opened up the educational
box."[20] The radical alternative was to reconstruct the organization so that a few
schools stayed open from February 7-25 (to provide all students one day of regular experience per week) but to close most buildings and rely on other instructional methods including extensive use of television, radio, field trips, and nonschool facilities. The School Without Schools plan was presented and approved
by the Columbus Board of Education on January 31, 1977. Board members
were assured that emergency legislation would allow the Columbus schools to
close down most operations yet receive state aid reimbursement as if normal
education were occurring. The legislation, Senate Bill 51, was passed on February 2, 1977. School districts were allowed up to fifteen "emergency energy"
days of reimbursements.

The core of the crisis period for Columbus centered upon the decision to
initiate "School Without Schools."

Once the basic decision was made, a new school organization, designed to
cover all essential coordinative functions, was created. Several persons interviewed
for this study commented that the delineation of role responsibilities and functions to be administered were clearer during the month of February 1977 than
any time before or after. The "School Without Schools" *Handbook* is perhaps the
most comprehensive document ever created by a school system for the purpose
of describing how to adapt to a special crisis. For example, the document describes
the "mothballing" process as it effects each subject area rather than a general
statement of how to close a local school center. Specific directions were given
for such areas as physical education, drivers' education, trade, industry and agri-
culture, audiovisual, and art.

All local schools were affected by the "School Without Schools" reorganization. Eighteen of the 156 local schools conducted education in nonschool facilities. All other schools were clustered in relation to a host school where classes
were scheduled one day per week. During the other four days of the three weeks
which "School Without Schools" operated, each local school center adapted
according to its own organizational arrangement.

Although the highly touted "School Without Schools" was judged a successful crisis adaptation, several late February events raised the issue of whether the
planned effort was excessive. First, on Friday of the third week (February 18)
P.U.C.O. negated Columbia Gas of Ohio's existing 85 percent curtailment because
of the impact of the Emergency Natural Gas Act of 1977.[21] Under this act, the
president had authority to order transfers of interstate natural gas and to approve
sales of gas to interstate buyers at unregulated prices. By Tuesday, February 22,
Columbia Gas of Ohio raised its curtailment level to 50 percent of base allocation.

The second factor that made the third week of "School Without Schools" a questionable necessity was the weather. The average temperatures climbed into the mid-forties and low fifties and all snow accumulation disappeared. However, large bureaucratic organizations cannot easily plan or adapt on a daily basis. Once "School Without Schools" was operationalized, it would run the stipulated three weeks in February no matter what the actual weather or energy fuel situation was.

As an additional safeguard against winter severity and fuel shortage, Columbus planners had modified the school calendar so that "spring break" immediately followed the third week of "School Without Schools." Again, the actual weather may not have necessitated the schools' being closed that week (February 28-March 4) as temperatures reached the fifties.

Aftermath of Crisis

In both Cincinnati and Columbus, the preoccupation with winter crisis ended around the first of March 1977. It was at this time that average temperatures rose to freezing and less than an inch of snow remained on the ground in either location. As a Columbus central office administrator noted, "When the last snowflake fell we got back to the jobs of 'normal' crisis. It's amazing how quickly and completely you can forget."

In reality, of course, the adverse effects of winter 1977 remained well into May. Although the effects lacked the visibility of an icy road or cold building, the impact on the school system was still severe. One such impact was the heating season designated for natural fuel allocations by the public utilities. Although the most severe curtailment levels of 85 percent were removed from the school base allocations by late February, the overall nature of the gas shortage remained. Columbus, for example, would remain under reduced heating season allocations from Columbia Gas of Ohio until April 3, 1977. Although the dramatic characteristics of winter 1977 were removed, both school systems continued to live with the fact that 70 percent of their local schools relied on a fuel in short supply.

Another aspect of winter 1977 that continued to influence both school systems long after the warming days of March was the attempt to justify emergency actions to state agencies. As we will see later, there was considerable negotiation with the State Department of Education in the areas of "crisis days" and "emergency transportation."

In spite of the carryover effects of winter, both school systems had replaced the harsh memories of weather with another form of crisis by April 1977.

Cincinnati

The spring of 1977 was a traumatic time for the Cincinnati schools. Less than a month after the winter adaptation effort the teachers' federation and board of education reached an impasse over finances. On March 14, 1977, fourteen days after the energy concern "ended," Cincinnati schools were embroiled in a familiar type of crisis. On face value, the issue had a familiar ring to many large school districts. The Cincinnati board and superintendent declared a zero budget as of December, 1977, with no contingency funds and a projected shortage of $10 to $15 million for the 1978 budget (of an $88.4 million 1977 budget with an addition of $7.3 million from a 1976 surplus).

On the other hand the teachers demanded a 16.3 percent cost-of-living raise, limits on class size, "more voice in school politics," and, later, binding arbitration of grievances.[22]

The result of these positions was a nationally visible teacher strike which lasted from April 13 to May 9 and ended with the power of the teachers transferred from an NEA affiliate to one associated with AFL-CIO. An interesting aspect of the fight over funds is that neither the Board of Education nor teacher federation cited the crisis of winter 1977 as contributing to or affecting the strike in any way.

The spring of 1977 was also the time that Cincinnati schools received a favorable judgment in their legal suit against the present financing scheme in the state of Ohio. Like many other states, Ohio public education is underfinanced and discriminatory to school districts without a strong local tax base.[23] Cincinnati schools brought suit against the State Superintendent of Public Instruction, on an equal yield type argument.[24] In the case, the civil court judge hearing the suit ruled for the Cincinnati schools that the present legislation for and method of financing was inadequate and discriminatory. Further, the judge gave specific directions to the legislature, including consideration of full state funding.

An energy-related decision which affected both the Cincinnati and the Columbus schools also occurred in the summer. The P.U.C.O. further clarified the relation of public schools to curtailment of natural gas policies. Although schools were not placed in the exempt "human needs" category, they were allowed a more favored status on new priority classifications for curtailment.[25] The impact of the new classification was that public schools were assured of at least 70 percent of their heating season base allocations of natural gas. Because base allocation remains calculated on old use figures and the overall conservation efforts in both systems, "70 percent" represents more than the pre-1977 winter needs for natural gas. In effect, the P.U.C.O. ruling told the schools that there would be no real shortage in their critical energy supply, no matter how severe the 1978 winter.

Finally, Cincinnati and Columbus faced an unexpected, energy-related issue in winter 1978. A national coal strike, coupled with strange weather, created a circumstance of electrical energy shortage.[26] In relation to this study and the previous winter it is important to note that the schools were largely unprepared for this new crisis. Indeed, many of the compensations for the natural gas shortage crisis contributed to the shortage problems of winter 1978.

Columbus

In Columbus, memories of winter 1977 disappeared under the new press of court-ordered desegregation. The basic mechanisms to effect compliance were busing and the "clustering" of certain attendance areas. The following identifies the cluster concept to desegregate pupils and teachers at the elementary level.

> The cluster concept involves the identification of two or more present elementary school attendance areas and the reorganization of the identified area into a single attendance area with more than one school serving the enlarged attendance area. Under this concept, each school in the enlarged attendance area would have some but not all of the elementary grade levels in attendance. As an example, a two school cluster might provide for the assignment of kindergarten pupils to their previous home school, the assignment of all pupils in grades 1, 2, and 3 in the enlarged area to School A, and the assignment of all pupils in grades 4, 5, and 6 to school B. In addition, the cluster plan anticipates the closing of some schools in clusters which include more than two present elementary attendance areas.

> Within a cluster, teachers assigned to a school which will include the grade level, or any part of the grade level, they are assigned to teach at the time of reorganization shall be assigned to that school. Teachers assigned to a school which will not include the grade level they are assigned to teach at the time of reorganization and teachers assigned to a school which will be closed shall be placed in a staff reduction pool for that cluster. Teachers in the staff reduction pool will then elect the school of their choice within the cluster and indicate a grade level preference. Election will begin with the most senior teacher. . . .[27]

Columbus personnel interviewed were of the opinion that the "cluster" organization which occurred throughout School Without Schools was *not* related to the court's decision for implementing desegregation.

A second issue of school system organization occurred in late summer. The acting superintendent of schools was elevated to a permanent status. In close proximity to the role change was the "most massive reorganization of the central office which Columbus had undergone in twenty years."[28] Throughout the fall of 1977 many central office administrators attempted to adjust to new functions and responsibilities.

In summary, the fact that the winter 1977 crisis was "forgotten" soon after the cold weather abated can be attributed to two reasons. First, both school systems faced other crises in the spring. Apparently the trauma of a teacher strike or court-ordered desegregation effort is intense enough to rank alongside weather in affecting policymaking on a situational basis. In spring, summer, and fall the technical problems of coping with fuel shortage and heating needs are replaced with normal, human-oriented issues.

Second, winter 1977 was forgotten when the P.U.C.O. established guidelines which made extreme shortages of natural gas again seem improbable. The crisis mentality of winter 1977 was partly the constant threat of absolute shortage in heating fuel. The P.U.C.O. guarantee of at least 70 percent base allocation allowed educators to think again of an energy shortage as a manageable, predictable problem.

Summary

The precrisis period contained several major events which helped shape winter 1977 policymaking. Making 1972 the benchmark year, the combination of public utility and state regulatory commission actions created the policy meanings of "short supply" in natural gas resources. The essential vehicles to establish a sense of limit to availability were the base allocation seasons and plans for specific curtailment amounts.

The role of the State Department of Education established the precedent that energy resource availability and natural gas shortages were legitimate matters of educational concern.

The P.U.C.O. Report of May 1976 was important in creating the impression that extreme natural gas shortage was an illusion. School officials were indirectly assured that their intensive conservation efforts during the latter part of 1975 and early 1976 were sufficient to avoid the crisis of fuel unavailability.

The final event of the precrisis period was the shattering of the illusion that the winter of 1977 was manageable in terms of conventional assumptions based upon prior assurances when curtailment amounts were increased.

The core of the winter 1977 crisis occurred in January and February, and the adaptation of the Columbus and Cincinnati schools presents two different stories.

Cincinnati limped through the first three weeks of January before being forced to admit that normal routines and standard operating procedures would not work. An effort to establish a day-to-day form of planning was shattered by ever growing shortages of available fuel. Finally, transportation and local school reorganization involving select pupils and staff in large gas user schools were initiated. The host-guest plan and other modifications generally minimized the dramatic abnormal efffects of winter 1977 to one-fourth of the pupils in the school system.

The Columbus story began with the natural gas curtailment that destroyed the illusions of fuel availability and a manageable crisis. Facing a seemingly insurmountable set of circumstances, Columbus school officials spent most of January attempting to pursuade the state-wide policy agendas of the legislature, SDE, and governor's office that emergency relief was necessary. Once assured that emergency relief was forthcoming (emergency days), the Columbus schools created an elaborate three-week plan for total reorganization of the system for the duration of the crisis. The month of February was characterized by the implementation of "School Without Schools," a plan which presented Columbus pupils with a set of radically different educational services and activities.

The aftermath of winter 1977 found that the unprecedented crisis was "forgotten as the last snowflake fell," although both school systems remained (and do today) dependent upon natural gas for winter operations. However, both school systems became embroiled in a variety of normal crises during the spring of 1977. Cincinnati forgot winter due to the combination of a nineteen-day teacher strike and presenting a successful court suit challenging Ohio's method of state aid financing.

Columbus schools spent the spring of 1977 implementing court-ordered desegregation plans and adjusting to a new superintendent of schools.

Another aspect of the aftermath created the impression that winter 1977 crisis was a one-time phenomenon. This was the ruling of P.U.C.O. that no school gas allotment could be curtailed by more than 30 percent of the base allocation. Both Columbus and Cincinnati were operating at less than the amount specified as maximum curtailment. Thus, the impression that both natural gas availability and sustained facility heating were possible by manageable planning was recreated.

The final event of the aftermath occurred in winter 1978 when coal shortages demonstrated again the temporariness of conventional planning assumptions in energy related types of crisis.

The reader now has a broad overview of the key events which describe the core of the 1977 winter crisis. The rest of the text is devoted to in-depth analysis of major variables which contributed to how Columbus and Cincinnati schools responded to the crisis. We start with those environmental variables which contribute to both inter- and intraorganization variation; severe winter, fuel availability, and policy environment.

Notes

1. In contrast to Columbus, there was little formal recognition of energy as an educational concern for Cincinnati until spring 1975. At that time, the public utility serving the schools (Cincinnati Gas and Electric) notified its customers to expect a 28 percent curtailment of natural gas for winter 1976 base allocations.

2. In winters 1975 and 1976 Columbus schools were under 40 percent curtailment for "large user" natural gas facilities. Cincinnati large user schools were under 20 percent curtailment in winter 1976.

3. Columbus officials were so convinced of their security that they refused to purchase an additional supply of natural gas which unexpectedly came available in late summer 1976.

4. Columbus schools overconsumed their November allotment by one-third, even with all-out conservation efforts.

5 Columbia Gas of Ohio had appealed to P.U.C.O. to raise curtailments thirteen days earlier but were denied.

6. Resolution on Energy Allocation, Ohio State Board of Education, adopted November 11, 1974.

7. Memo, Coordinator, Pupil Transportation Branch to Asst. Supt. for Human Resources, January 15, 1977; Board of Education *Minutes*, January 18, 1977, pp. 23-25, indicate that more than half the Cincinnati pupils were absent during the time transportation was not provided or was somewhat curtailed.

8. Quoted in article, "Energy Crisis Hits City Schools' Purse," *Cincinnati Post*, February 14, 1977. However, Cincinnati did ultimately declare four "emergency energy days" for junior high and secondary schools affected by the host-guest pairing plan during February. Under the double schedule both hosts and guests received four-hour school days. While four hours make a legal elementary holiday it does not meet requirements for secondary. The four hours do count toward a minimum of twenty-five secondary hours per week. Thus five four-hour days are equal to four five-hour days (the minimum requirement for a secondary day is five hours).

9. Since September 14, 1975, Cincinnati schools had been notified by their public utility that twenty large user facilities could be curtailed 28 percent in case of an emergency.

10. Open memo, James Jacobs, "Alternative Plans for School Scheduling through Friday, February 4, 1977," dated January 31, 1977.

11. Memo, Couzins to Fields, February 4, 1977. Metro buses would not commit services beyond the two schedule splits in the original plan.

12. Letter, Louis Klug to Couzins, February 8, 1977. Memo, Couzins to Holloway, February 8, 1977. Another modification was the absorption of city-wide alternative curriculum programs into their neighborhood school.

13. Memo, Couzins to Holloway, February 8, 1977. Memo, Holloway to Jacobs, February 9, 1977, citing daily extra costs as $1,900.

14. Letter from Rev. Duane Holm to Cincinnati Board of Education and Queen City Metro, February 7, 1977.

15. The committee, consisting of seven central office administrators, four principals, three teachers, four classified employees, and two members of the P.T.A., had been in existence for three years.

16. "Investigate the feasibility of establishing joint secondary school organizations whereby some schools could be closed and others used on a split schedule basis," point no. 9, interoffice communication memorandum from Fulton to John Ellis, January 7, 1977.

17. The actors of the Gas, Inc., were Jerry Jordan and Jonathan Airey of the Vorys, Sater, Seymour and Pease law firm, Gene Brasel of Brasel and Brasel Oil Company, and Jack Connell of Clinton Oil Company. Mr. Jordan headed the initiative to coordinate logistics of securing gas which involved the cooperation of Federal Power Commission, P.U.C.O., Columbia Gas of Ohio, Columbia Gas Transmission Company, and several independent producers.

18. Spot checks of pupil attendance found absences running 4 to 28 percent above normal, memo from pupil personnel, January 19, 1977.

19. To finish the heating season (April 3), memo, Calvin Smith to John Ellis, January 27, 1977.

20. Fred Hechinger, "School without Schools" *Saturday Review*, April 30, 1977, pp. 13, 16.

21. *Congressional Quarterly Weekly Report* 35:6 (February 5, 1977), 191-195. This changed the legal constraint whereby *interstate* gas was controlled by the Federal Power Commission to a well-head price that could not exceed $.53 per MCF, but *intrastate* gas was not so regulated. That's why Columbus schools' self-help gas program was from instate wells at $2.90 per MCF. The Emergency Natural Gas Act allowed all interstate gas prices to be unregulated until July 31, 1977.

22. Report on 1977 teacher strike in Cincinnati prepared by Sally Roush. Special thanks for her assistance in this description. Some teachers pointed to a State Department of Education report released March 17 as generating broad support for militant teacher action. The report charged Cincinnati schools as being "administrator heavy," citing the gain of thirty-four administrators during the past five years while the system lost 15,661 students and 184 teachers.

23. There is a double bind of meeting minimum state standards for accreditation which stipulates type and extent of expenditures and that receiving foundation monies is dependent upon a minimum contribution of local citizen effort. City school systems also suffer loss of education dollars in subsidizing "shared services" with other municipal governments. In fall 1977 thirty-six of Ohio's 617 local districts filed for bankruptcy.

24. The Ohio legislation for financing at the time of this study was Senate Bill 170. The "equal yield" foundation formula type of allocation was subsidized at 17 percent. See Jerry Steck, "Effect of Ohio's Guaranteed Equal Yield Formula upon Equalization of Basic State Aid and Revenue Per Pupil for Equal Tax Effort," doctoral dissertation, Miami University, 1977.

25. P.U.C.O., *Interim Orders*, issued March 16, 1977, March 30, 1977, and May 11, 1977, in P.U.C.O. Case No. 75-568-GA-AGC.

26. The large percentage of the type of resources used by Ohio public utilities to generate electrical power is coal. In December 1977 two days of rain followed by extremely cold temperatures froze utility coal piles into huge, unusable pyramids. In the later stages of winter 1978, overall coal shortages necessitated electrical curtailment. This and natural gas will probably be the fuels involved in any continuing energy shortage crises for schools in the future.

27. *Memorandum of Agreement*, signed by teachers June 27, 1977; signed by board July 5, 1977. The original case was *Penick and others v. Columbus Board of Education and others*.

28. Personal interview, November 11, 1977.

3

Severe Weather and Fuel Availability

A key element in understanding the inter- and intraorganizational variations of how Columbus and Cincinnati schools responded to the winter of 1977 is to understand what "severe weather" and "fuel availability" meant to the case study context. This chapter is concerned with two of the environmental variables which are hypothesized to effect the total milieu of crisis response. The basic question of the severe weather variable is the extent to which Columbus weather conditions approximated Cincinnati conditions prior to and during winter 1977.

There are some basic questions concerning the fuel availability variable. What was the effect of existing intergovernmental arrangements? What was the effect of intraorganization decisions taken prior to winter 1977 and during winter 1977? Answering these questions provides a broad framework for the detailed study of how Columbus and Cincinnati actually differed or varied in their planning and crisis response.

The Severe Weather

Both Cincinnati and Columbus, Ohio, have climates described as continental, with a wide range in temperature. The average date for the first freeze of fall is October 25 for Cincinnati residents, while Columbus's first fall freeze is normally October 31. In the spring, the last freeze usually occurs on April 10 for the city of Cincinnati and April 16 in Columbus.

To understand the severity of the 1977 winter it must be recognized that the 1976 winter was characterized as warmer than normal with considerably less precipitation in both cities. During 1976, February and March temperatures in Cincinnati were 9° and 7° above normal. Total annual precipitiation was 30.24 inches, which is 9.2 inches below normal. Similarly, Columbus temperatures for February and March 1976 were 7° and 6° above normal with annual precipitation 31.85 inches (5.1 inches below the mean).

The "hot and dry" winter of 1976 stands in sharp contrast to the severity of winter 1977. In Cincinnati, the average temperatures for each of the twelve months of the 1976-77 calendar year were below normal. Particularly low average temperatures occurred in November and December 1976 and January 1977 when departures from normal were 7°, 5°, and 16°. A statistic called heating degree days specifies the daily number of degrees Fahrenheit that are needed to be added to the average daily temperature to achieve 65°. Monthly and yearly calculations of heating degree day normals are derived from data gathered from 1941 to 1970. In the 1976-77 year Cincinnati was an unprecedented 829 degree days above normal. Even more significantly, the month of January 1977 alone accounted for a deviation of 516 heating degree days.

In Columbus, the colder than average weather began in July 1976 and became progressively colder through January 1977. For example, October 1976 averaged 8° below normal: November, 9°: December 1976 was 10° and January an unprecedented 18° below average temperature. Total Columbus heating degree days for the 1976-77 year were 955 degree days above normal. January 1977 accounted for 524 of the degree day deviation.

All of the above data lead to the conclusion that winter 1977 was truly without precedent in terms of actual coldness and heating needs. The core of the crisis from a climatological perspective was January 1977. This perspective is interesting in terms of the concentrated adaptation efforts taken by Columbus and Cincinnati schools which occurred in February 1977. While February 1977 temperatures averaged 3° below normal for both cities, heating degree day needs were only sixty-one above normal in Cincinnati and ninety-nine in Columbus for the month. In effect, the truly severe immediate impact of winter 1977 had passed before concentrated crisis response occurred in either system.

Another major contributor to the severity of winter 1977 was the lulling aspect of the previous winter. This gave policymakers both a false picture of energy needs and a false sense of security in their ability to adapt. We can understand and appreciate the dilemma of energy suppliers and users in 1977 when the 1976 heating degree day totals were 522 below normal in Cincinnati and 275 below normal in Columbus. It was impossible for a planner to predict the winter of 1977 from 1976 winter data. Further, even long-range trends gave little clue that 1977 would be so severe.

Natural Gas Fuel Availability

It could be argued that the weather alone was responsible for the crisis nature of winter 1977. However, the dramatically increased heating needs were coupled with basic problems of delivery and supply.

In this case study, fuel availability seemed to be a function of three basic determinants: *interorganizational policies* in effect which stipulated (a) base allocation levels of natural gas which could be secured, (b) curtailments of supply which would occur in emergencies, and (c) patterns of internal fuel distribution and gaining extra amounts in emergencies; *interorganizational arrangements* of the public utility distributor to its supplier(s) of natural gas; and *intraorganizational decisions* taken by the school systems to conserve natural gas and reduce consumption.

To understand heating fuel availability one must understand the relationship among the Cincinnati and Columbus schools and the Columbia Gas System.[1] The System is an "interconnected conglomerate" which provides natural gas to both the cities under study, as well as many other areas of the eastern United States.[2] Natural gas is brought to Ohio by the Columbia Gas Transmission Company but the method of distributing gas to Cincinnati and Columbus is different. Columbus schools receive gas from a retail distributor (part of the parent Columbia Gas System) called Columbia Gas of Ohio, Inc.[3] On the other hand, Cincinnati schools receive gas from Cincinnati Gas and Electric Company, which is an independent utility.[4] Cincinnati Gas and Electric (hereafter CG and E) receives its natural gas directly from Columbia Gas Transmission Company as a wholesale market.

The importance of the relationship of the natural gas distributor (serving the schools) to its source of gas supply was emphasized during the 1977 winter, particularly as it created differences in service between CG and E and Columbia Gas of Ohio, Inc., and their respective customers. The most visible differences were the number of times a utility appeared before the state regulatory commission to appeal existing rate structures. Columbia Gas of Ohio, Inc., charged Columbus schools twice the dollar amount for a thousand cubic feet (called an MCF) of natural gas than that charged to Cincinnati schools by CG and E for a similar amount.[5] The 1977 winter showed that the availability of fuel itself was somewhat dependent upon the utility arrangement a school system was under. Reversing what might have been expected to be found, the wholesale market (CG and E) was able to deliver better natural gas services to its customers during the 1977 crisis than Columbia Gas of Ohio, Inc. (as an integral retail market). Although the particular reasons for variation of delivery, such as the number and type of customers served (or the internal organizational arrangements of the two utilities), were beyond this study, the overall variation as impact upon availability of fuel to schools was highly visible. Simply put, Cincinnati schools were less hampered by the lack of fuel from their public utility (in terms of when curtailments were imposed and extent of deprivation) than Columbus schools.[6] It might be concluded that the "sense of crisis" which motivated Columbus school officials to take major actions to find new sources of natural gas (while Cincinnati did not) was due, in part, to the more stringent conditions of unavailability imposed by Columbia Gas of Ohio, Inc.

A second, critical understanding of heating fuel availability concerns the role of the state regulatory commission in relation to the distribution of existing fuels. The Public Utilities Commission of Ohio (hereafter P.U.C.O.) was responsible[7] for legal interpretation of all interorganizational policy concerning the allocation, curtailment, distribution, or redistribution of energy resources. P.U.C.O. duties include hearing utility rate price increase requests and approving allocation and curtailment plans for individual utilities. During the winter of 1977, P.U.C.O. gained high political visibility when the normal mechanisms for making decisions were overloaded by the dynamics of crisis.

Compared to other state regulatory commissions, Ohio P.U.C.O. has been classified an "imitator" rather than a leader. Joskow's[8] classification of utility commission roles (in establishing base rates in times of disequilibrium) describes imitator states as monitoring activities in other states and, when adopting, cite leader commissions as precedent for their state decision. Similarly, a 1972 survey of conservation and curtailment conducted by the National Association of Regulatory Commissions found that "Ohio . . . relied on the interstate pipeline network and local distributors to take the initiative in the handling of gas shortage problems. . . ."[9]

The contribution of P.U.C.O. to the variations of intergovernmental planning and school crisis response cannot be overstated. First, the imitator role of the Ohio Commission meant that P.U.C.O. was never "on top of" the winter 1977 crisis. Consequently, regulatory decisions made prior to and during the period of severe fuel shortage were reactionary and "knee jerk." As will be discussed in detail later, the legitimization of utility curtailment plans and the subsequent "emergency" curtailments of winter 1977 provide visible examples of inconsistency and indecision.

A second impact of P.U.C.O. concerned the specific decisions made in relation to Ohio public schools as a "special class" of gas users and those decisions that affected the customers of a particular utility. As will be noted in upcoming discussion, the P.U.C.O. decisions on "human need" classification of schools to achieve exemption from gas curtailments and decisions about the approval of original curtailment plans (or emergency modifications) revealed no uniformity.[10] The "rationality" of certain decisions has less impact on particular variation among schools and their distributors than the fact there were no standard criteria for judging continuity from system to system or time to time. This helped to create the unsatisfactory policy condition of P.U.C.O. judgments about particular energy conditions being treated as "precedent" as other utilities and schools tried to anticipate and "juggle" their own situations.

Interorganizational Policies

A specific comparison of Columbus and Cincinnati schools showed that both general and special winter 1977 related differences were found in policies about base allocations, curtailments, and fuel distribution.

The term "base allocation" means the method and amount of natural gas which the utilities will provide to public schools as a domestic user.[11] In 1972 CG and E calculated the base allocation for Cincinnati on the actual consumption of natural gas by the twenty largest gas user schools over a twelve-month period. In contrast, Columbia Gas of Ohio, Inc., calculated consumption of natural gas by forty-five Columbus schools for twenty-four months between 1972 and 1974. The Columbus school base allocation was based upon the maximum twelve-month usage during the two-year time frame. The two base allocations established in the early 1970s remained in effect until the 1977 winter crisis.[12]

Another area of distinct variation between the effects of intergovernmental policies on Columbus and Cincinnati schools was the area of fuel curtailments. Columbia Gas of Ohio, Inc., filed an initial curtailment plan with P.U.C.O. in July 1972. The plan established that natural gas would be allocated (and, if necessary curtailed) by a heating and nonheating season.[13] The effect of this curtailment plan on the Columbus schools' effort to adapt to the 1977 winter was profound. Most strategy was directed to the issue of how to survive until the formal end of the heating season (April 3), when new allocation calculations would come into effect. This designation of fuel availability, rather than the impact of severe weather, became a cornerstone of Columbus long-range planning.

It was not until June 1975 that CG and E filed a curtailment plan with P.U.C.O. that would affect Cincinnati schools. Several specific and significant differences highlighted the CG and E curtailment as it would affect schools compared to the existing plan of Columbia Gas of Ohio, Inc.: (a) if industrial users would be curtailed before domestic, (b) if curtailment would be applied to a "broadened base,"[14] (c) if initial base allocation amounts would be used to calculate curtailment amounts, (d) if minimum amounts for "plant protection" would be guaranteed, and (e) if there could be "carryover"[15] from one season to another. Each of these five points distinguished policy areas where the Columbus schools were impacted differently by curtailment than was the Cincinnati school system.[16]

A final area of potential variation in interorganizational policies which could affect fuel availability concerns how natural gas can be utilized by a particular school system and whether schools have the right to try to find additional amounts.

Both Cincinnati and Columbus were told by their respective utilities (and approved by P.U.C.O.) that they could "pool" the natural gas accounts for their large user schools. In Cincinnati, the gas allocated to the twenty largest user schools (called category 2) could be used in any way the local district saw fit. For example, if a large user school had been converted to another type of fuel, its gas allocation would not be lost but could be used by other facilities in the system (as long as the total "pooled" allocation was not exceeded, the use was at the discretion of the school system). Columbus provides another type of example of the pooling concept in operation. In this case, the particular limits of base allocation for forty-five big user schools were too stringent in terms of actual need and use of natural gas. In this case, gas pooled from other accounts (for example, "small users" which did not exceed 1,000 MCFs) could be used to compensate the large school needs.[17] If, at this point, the reader is getting a feeling that the whole process of determining "concrete guidelines" for fuel availability is somewhat suspect and illusory, the politicized understanding of this policy phenomenon is being accomplished.

Both Cincinnati and Columbus schools were allowed to attempt to secure emergency amounts of natural gas under the self-help concept.[18] At the time P.U.C.O. guidelines were released (in late March 1976), self-help gas was seen as a vehicle whereby select users could substitute independent sources of gas for normal base allocations. The guidelines stipulated that any public utility in Ohio could enter into an arrangement with one or more of its customers (that is, Columbus or Cincinnati schools alone or a number of the school systems in a metropolitan area could enter into a self-help arrangement) to transport independent gas from production point to point of consumption. Although amounts received could not exceed a customer's base allocation for any month,[19] the most important aspect of self-help was its virtual immunity to curtailment.[20]

From a policy standpoint, self-help gas was seen as only possible for "rich" users who had their own wells or large amounts of capital to invest in high-risk ventures.[21] However, the 1977 winter emphasized the enormous potential long-term benefits for those select users who could develop independent sources of gas. First, Ohio self-help gas usually comes from in-state wells rather than being transported from Louisiana or Texas. Intrastate rates are perceived as having a better chance of becoming stable, compared to rates for interstate networks (like Columbia Gas System). Interstate rates could reflect customer costs of Arab and/or Alaskan prices and possible congressional deregulation of existing price controls.[22]

In summary, the availability of natural gas for heating of the schools was directly affected by the existing intergovernmental policies which purport to determine base allocation, curtailment, internal distribution, and securing other supplies. The Cincinnati and Columbus data suggest that extreme variation in policy guides occur in the areas of how base allocations are established, interpreted and in the specification of curtailment. The policies in these areas are both a function of the particular plan filed by the utility and approved by the regulatory commission and the politicized nature of the phenomenon.

On the other hand, the policy guides for internal distribution of natural gas and securing new, emergency amounts were the same for each school system. In this case, variations were a function of district decision-making, not the stipulations of intergovernmental policies.

A second way to distinguish the variation of intergovernmental policies on fuel availability is the extent of decision autonomy or discretion implied in a particular guideline. In this study, neither Columbus nor Cincinnati had control of curtailment mandates. The establishment of base allocation appears to give the school systems little discretion, but, as we will see later, there is much room for "creative accounting."

Finally, the policies concerning internal distribution and securing of emergency (self-help) supplies allow the local districts wide discretion. We now turn to a second area which affects variation in fuel availability—interorganizational arrangements of supply and demand.

Intergovernmental Arrangements

This study found that the particular fuel arrangement between a school system and its public utility was a function of (1) the relation of the utility to its major supplier (in these cases, the Columbia Gas Transmission Company) and (2) the relative importance that a particular utility assigned to different classifications of users.

Information gathered from indirect sources[23] concerning the role of Columbia Gas Transmission Company as major supplier of public utilities suggests two conclusions about intergovernmental arrangements. First, Cincinnati Gas and Electric, the independent wholesale market, seemed to receive "better treatment" in terms of guaranteed flow of the gas resources than Columbia Gas of Ohio, Inc., the retail market. This conclusion is based upon a comparison of actual and anticipated curtailment practices prior to and during winter 1977. For example, on April 30, 1975, CG and E was told by Columbia Gas Transmission to expect a 28 percent curtailment of gas supplies for the 1975-76 winter. At approximately the same time (August 30, 1975), Columbia Gas of Ohio notified Columbus schools to expect a 40 percent curtailment for the 1975-76 winter. There seem to be two possible conclusions: either the Transmission Company curtailed an additional 12 percent for its retail outlet or Columbia Gas of Ohio readjusted the 12 percent to other users in its distribution net. In either case the "wholesale" relationship seems less punitive to the school system at the receiving end. A second conclusion about intergovernmental arrangement is that the interstate transmitters of gas will probably gain increasing power to determine fuel availability in the future.

Orders 533 and 533A of the Federal Power Commission, issued December 16, 1976, were important for they established guidelines for obtaining self-help and other emergency gas that was available via interstate pipelines. Obviously, both Cincinnati and Columbus utilities and school systems were affected by the ruling, for Columbia Gas Transmission Company is their major interstate carrier of natural gas. Emergency interstate gas could be obtained under the following conditions; if use requirements (for example, of schools) exceeded 50 MCF on a peak day; if a purchase agreement did *not* include an indefinite pricing clause; if Columbia Transmission would charge 22.21 cents per MCF for transportation, plus an additional 2.54 cents per MCF where gas is delivered into a production facility; if Columbia Transmission would keep 3.1 percent of the total volume to compensate for shrinkage; if an affidavit were signed that the gas was not for resale.

The policy implications of FPC orders 533 and 533A were not to be understood until the aftermath of winter 1977. At that time (spring 1977) the meaning of certain stipulations and the growing decision role of Columbia Gas Transmission Company became increasingly important to the growing political controversy of self-help gas availability in Ohio.

A third conclusion about variation in intergovernmental arrangements concerns the particular user classification which a public utility uses to determine priorities in allocating available fuel. As noted earlier, all users are classified either industrial or domestic. Domestic is further divided into residential, commercial, and commercial of a "residential or human needs"category, although that category includes apartments, hospitals, jails, nursing homes, hotels, and motels.[24] The customers in this category are exempt from curtailment mandates of natural gas. As will be dicussed later, the SDE was involved in an unsuccessful effort to have all schools placed in the exempt categories.[25] Because of their nonexempt nature, schools must compete with other gas users for fuel. The success of the "competition" is reflected in the curtailment priorities of a particular utility's plan. This becomes very confusing in that, beyond the classification of industrial and commercial user, there is also a distinction between *end use*, which considers type of use (for example, to fire boilers) and *pro rata*, which is a classification of whole categories (for example, the schools). It is possible for a school system to be classified under both end use and pro rata classifications in a particular utility's priority system of availability and curtailment. Under this double kind of priority setting a school may have a low, "safe" category classification (pro rata) but a high, first to be curtailed (end use) priority. Both affect the operational meaning of whether fuel is actually available for a particular school system.

In summary, one should think of intergovernmental arrangements that affect fuel availability in a larger context than the local public utility. Data seem to suggest that control of interstate transmission of natural gas did and will have a major impact upon variation in distribution (and use) practices.

Intraorganizational Decisions

The last major policy areas affecting variation in the availability of natural gas fuel were energy decisions made within the school systems of Columbus and Cincinnati. These intraorganizational decisions include conservation efforts taken prior to winter 1977 and emergency actions taken during the 1977 crisis.

Columbus schools began to think seriously about energy conservation in 1973, and Cincinnati schools, a year later. Although both systems had technical personnel in plant operation and maintenance who were concerned prior to the above dates, most of the school system was not. However, the growing interest of the Ohio State Department of Education in energy conservation[26] and how schools should prepare for a crisis[27] triggered a general reaction in the Columbus and Cincinnati districts. The specific reactions of the Columbus schools were to complete an exhaustive facility by facility fuel consumption analysis (October 1975) and prepare the following general conservation guide for all local schools:

1. Reduce boiler water temperatures to the minimum level necessary to maintain 68 degree temperatures in the classroom.

2. Reduce hot water temperatures to the 130 degree level at schools with cafeterias and to 110 degrees in all other school facilities.

3. Convene the Advisory Council for the purpose of gathering energy conservation recommendations for implementation at your school.

4. Heating—General:

    a. Lower thermostat settings to "sweater comfort" heating. Encourage students, teachers and school employees to dress accordingly.

    b. Reduce fresh air ventilation to the minimum required by state and local codes.

    c. Operate boiler(s) at as high a load/capacity ratio as possible. Two boilers at one-half capacity use more gas than one at full cap.

5. Effective Use of Heating Equipment:

    a. Control room temperatures with thermostats, not by opening windows.

    b. Avoid setting a room thermostat higher than the temperature ultimately desired. This only overheats the room and wastes fuel.

    c. Set the thermostat as low as possible for as long as possible when an area is unoccupied.

    d. Avoid blocking heating vents or air return grills with furniture or drapes.

    e. Let sunlight into the building on cold days and keep it out on warm, humid days.

    f. Close drapes and blinds after school hours to reduce heat loss through window areas in winter and to keep heat out in summer.

    g. Limit the number of entrances used during arrival and departure hours: and, if possible, select those that face away from prevailing winds.

    h. Keep outside doors closed when not in use. If doorway has double doors, keep both sets closed.

6. Maintenance

    a. Clean or replace dirty furnace filters on a regular basis.

    b. Clean heat exchange surface or heating system to maintain heat transfer efficiency.

c. Check air/fuel ratios. A steady blue flame indicates proper adjustments.

d. Make a flue analysis. You may be losing too much fuel up the chimney.

e. Clean combustion air blower equipment regularly.

f. Treat boiler to minimize scaling—flush out boiler prior to start of heating season.

g. Inspect. all thermostats and other controls regularly for proper operation.

h. Provide for adequate combustion air in the boiler room. Examine the feasibility of introducing exhaust air from the classrooms into the boiler room to be used as preheated combustion air.

i. Check and replace washers in leaking hot and cold water faucets.

j. Reduce hot water temperature settings to the lowest acceptable level.

7. Other

a. Operate ventilation fans in kitchens and home economics rooms only when cooking equipment is in operation.

b. Seal all openings around windows and other places through which warm air could escape.

8. Lighting

a. Turn off both incandescent and fluorescent lights when they are not needed. New fluorescent bulbs take less energy to "warm-up" than did their predecessors: and research now indicates that energy is saved if fluorescent lights are turned off when they will not be in use for at least five minutes.

b. Instruct school custodians to turn off lights room by room as they complete their cleaning assignments.

c. Turn off banks of lights nearest the window when outside light is adequate.

d. Reduce the use of corridor lighting consistent with safety and security.

e. Clean light fixtures regularly and replace bulbs and tubes as needed.

f. Check into the feasibility of installing two or three separate lighting circuits for areas such as multipurpose rooms, where high levels of lighting are needed only periodically.

g. Decorate all rooms (walls, ceilings and floors) with lighter colors that reflect rather than absorb light.

h. Use time clocks or photocell switches to control needed outdoor lighting.[28]

Cincinnati schools followed the same type of interorganizational decision-making, but approximately a year later. It was not until the summer of 1976 that a complete internal fuel consumption analysis was completed. The following energy conservation checklist was given to all Cincinnati local schools and other facilities in the spring of 1976:

I. Heating

Reduce the largest single "block" of energy user by better supervision of the heating system.

A. Reduce heating in areas of the building used infrequently, i.e. restrooms and storage rooms—never above $60°$: auditoriums only up to $68°$ when in use.
B. Heat rooms to $68°$ when in use and reduce to $60°$ during vacant periods.
C. Heat gyms and other physical activity rooms $60°$-$65°$ when in use and $55°$ when not being used.
D. Control heat as body heat effects room temperatures; turn off heat so that at building closing time night temperatures have been reached.
E. Encourage the use of outside light and heat through radiation by opening window shades; conversely, in the heating season close interior shades on cloudy days to help insulate over windows.
F. Schedule second shift operations and maintenance work to start from darker parts of building and proceed to warmer more lighted areas.
G. Encourage the permit use of buildings during the heating season during daylight hours.
H. Publicize via the daily bulletin, energy saving measures and heating reductions in the building to stress wearing proper clothing. Ventilation and infiltration conservation measures, etc. Develop an energy saving attitude.
I. Operate only the boilers and pumps that are necessary and only at the times they are needed. One at 90 percent capacity is better than two at 45 percent.
J. Check boiler and chiller water daily to determine its chemical composition and add treatment if necessary.
K. Check flue gas analysis on a periodic basis to achieve proper stack temperature and gas composition.

II. Ventilation

Reduce outdoor air to the minimum required to balance the ventilating system.

A. Check all outdoor dampers to assure proper operations—when closed they should be air tight.
B. Inspect, clean, and/or replace all air filters—establish a schedule of inspection.
C. Use exhaust fans only when programs requiring them are operating—laboratories and food preparation areas. Control fans to operate at speeds and times compatible with the job.
D. Turn off ventilating system whenever building is not in use.

E. Reduce volume of air in toilet air exhausts to the minimum required and clean toilet areas more frequently to eliminate odors.

III. Infiltration

Reduce outdoor air infiltration by tightening window and door openings.

A. Cover broken or cracked window pane openings *immediately* and write a work order for repair.
B. Caulk cracks around window and door frames.
C. Seal windows and doors that are not used.
    Example: Fasten corridor windows that are used only for illumination so that they cannot be opened.
D. Check all operable windows to be certain cam latches are working properly and if they are equipped with sealing gaskets that they are in good condition.
E. Post instructions for occupants not to open operable windows while building is being heated.
F. Check all outside doors and door closers daily to be sure they operate properly and are correctly aligned. Repair immediately.
G. Adjust door closers to operate doors quicker and allow doors to open less wide.
H. Close doors: Do not allow any doors to be propped open at any time.

I V. Lighting

A planned program to turn lights on only when and where they are needed is an effective lighting usage program and thus an energy saver.

A. Place desks and other work surfaces in positions that will best utilize the installed lights.
B. Clean lamps regularly and check light output for efficient proper wattage.
C. Replace lamps, as needed, with high surge voltage type lamps.
D. Post charts near multiple light switches to identify which light or lights each switch controls and thus prevent trial and error switching.
E. Clean ceilings, walls, floors, and windows to improve reflective qualities.
F. Modify lamps: eliminate, reduce wattage, and/or change types to give necessary illumination. Substitute fluorescent desk lamps for overhead banks in offices.

V. Equipment

Efficiency of the operations of equipment means a great energy saving.

A. Clean and properly lubricate machinery to reduce excessive friction causing heat and energy loss.
B. Inspect and repair gaskets and valves on a regular basis.
C. Clean refrigeration condensers and coils, and insure sufficient air circulation around them in order that they may "breathe."
D. Use hot water sparingly.
E. Inspect and adjust tension and alignment of belts. Lubricate all moving parts according to the manufacturer's recommendations.

VI. Electric Power

There are numerous elements in a building that use electric power in addition to those already mentioned. If their use were reviewed and controlled, it would save energy.

A. Turn off automatic devices using electricity when they will be idle for extended periods of time: i.e.: refrigerated drinking fountains over weekends and holiday periods.
B. Impress clerical personnel that all electric business machines should be turned off at all times they are not in use. On-off switches should be marked so that they will be clearly seen when in the on position.
C. Know when your peak electric usage time occurs (rates are based on peak demand) and programs around such peaks to "level off" usage and save money.
D. Check electrical connections, contacts, line loads, etc., to increase efficiency as well as safety.
E. Keep records of maintenance checks, showing what is done, when, and the condition of the equipment when checked.
F. Central control of electrical outlets and lights.

VII. Domestic Hot Water

Fuel to heat water for domestic use is reported to cost about 15 percent of the fuel costs; any conservation saves fuel, water, and energy.

A. Inspect all water faucets and repair those that leak.
B. Regulate water temperatures to no more than 100° and boost temperature locally for kitchens and other areas where hotter water is needed: i.e.: kitchens. Deactivate this hotter water when kitchens are not in use.[29]

As emphasized in the section on intraorganizational arrangements of the Cincinnati and Columbus schools (pp. 51-80) the elaborate conservation plans were for the use of technicians and had little impact on the practicing administrator or teachers of either system.

It seems clear that neither Columbus nor Cincinnati schools made intraorganizational energy decisions with any real sense of urgency about fuel availability. The combination of "creative" base allocation adjustments and a general "tightening" of technical aspects of energy conservation seemed to be enough to meet anticipated curtailments from the utilities. Indeed, internal consumption analyses verified that the 28 and 40 percent curtailments of the 1976 winter could and were being made without large-scale retrofitting[30] of facilities or other major cost outlays. There seemed little need to engage in extensive, comprehensive efforts "to make every member of the school system a conscious, continuous practitioner of energy conservation."[31]

In summary, intraorganizational decision-makers in both systems were driven by the need to conserve enough fuel to meet the assumed curtailment levels to be imposed by the public utilities. A major contributor to the true crisis for the 1977 winter was the fact that prior to that time the schools *were* practicing enough conservation to meet the assumed guarantee of availability. Columbus schools, for example, reduced their consumption of natural gas from 79,925,780 MCFs in 1974 to 74,646,600 MCFs in 1975 to 62,959,800 MCFs in 1976 and were publicly cited by Columbus Gas of Ohio as an exemplary, energy efficient school system.[32] It is not surprising that both school systems were unprepared for the dramatic curtailments and unavailability of fuel which occurred in winter 1977.

Summary

The availability of natural gas fuel in winter 1977 was a function of existing intergovernmental policies, intergovernmental arrangements, and intraorganizational decision-making. Perhaps exceeding the particular effects of the above functions were the overall policy roles of the public utilities and state regulatory commission in not anticipating the winter of 1977.

Specific variations in the crisis response of Columbus and Cincinnati schools can be traced to intergovernmental policies delineating the base allocation, curtailment, internal distribution, and securing of new emergency supplies of natural gas.

Second, interorganizational arrangements affect the availability of fuel. Of particular importance is the role of the gas supplier to the utilities and the particular classification of user priority in force by a utility.

Finally, intraorganizational decisions concerning the meaning of and need for energy conservation determine fuel availability.

Conclusions

The following conclusions address the four basic questions of the chapter.

First, winter 1977 was truly unprecedented in terms of severity. However, the severity affected both school systems the same way so that variations in policy response are not a function of unique conditions at one site. Severe weather has particular policy significance in relation to the ideas of heating degree days, wind chill (the combined effect of wind and cold upon people and windward walls of facilities), and snowfall/ice accumulation.

Second, a major determinant of fuel availability is the decision role and policy relationships of the public utilities and state energy regulatory commission *vis-à-vis* the public schools. In setting intergovernmental policies, the policy areas of establishing base allocation and internal distribution provide most school system discretion while curtailment is an area most controlled from the school decision-makers.

Third, intergovernmental arrangements affect variation in the school system's ability to secure natural gas. It was speculated this was due to (a) the power relation between the distributing public utility and its supplier and (b) the particular user classification established by the utility.

Fourth, intraorganizational decisions concerning school system conservation prior to and during winter 1977 affected the crisis nature of school response in securing available fuels.

These findings lend themselves to help the reader understand broad policy dynamics which set the stage for particular decision activities during winter 1977. The next chapter considers the third major variable affecting both inter- and intraorganizational variations in school system response to crisis: the environmental context.

Notes

1. Detailed information can be obtained from *Moody's Public Utility Manual*, 1976, pp. 475-487.

2. As a holding company, Columbia Gas System is composed of: a) the Columbia Gas and Electric Corporation; b) a service subsidiary (Columbia Gas Service Corporation); two transmission subsidiaries (Appalachian Transmission Co. and Columbia Gulf Transmission Co.) which form the Columbia Gas Transmission Corporation; c) seven distribution subsidiaries (operating in Ohio, Pennsylvania, Kentucky, New York, Virginia, West Virginia, and Maryland), the largest of which is Columbia Gas of Ohio, Inc.; d) another production and distribution subsidiary (Inland Gas Co.); e) two subsidiaries for exploring and developing hydrocarbons (Columbia Gas Development Corp. and Columbia Gas Development of Canada, Ltd.); f) a subsidiary to produce pipeline quality gas for reforming hydrocarbon feedstocks (Columbia Hydrocarbon Corporation); g) a subsidiary in coal gasification, acquisition and sale of coal (Columbia Coal Gasification Corp.); h) a subsidiary for propane and a liquid hydrocarbon reforming plant (Columbia LNG Corporation); i) a subsidiary to participate in the pipeline construction of arctic gas (Columbia Alaskan Gas Transmission Corp.). The System also owns 74 percent of Big Marsh Oil Company and Inland Gas Co.

3. Columbia Gas of Ohio, Inc., is the largest of seven distribution companies in the system. The 1,050,800 retail customers represent 59 percent of the domestic sales and 54 percent of the industrial sales of the entire system. Columbia Gas of Ohio is the direct distributor to 886,075 services.

4. Cincinnati Gas and Electric Company was once a subsidiary of Columbia Gas and Electric Corp. (until 1946) but is now the independent service for ten counties and 300,942 services in southwest Ohio. Although the majority of gas purchased is from the Columbia Gas Transmission Company, Cincinnati augments peak demand periods from its subsidiaries, the Union Light and Power Co. and the Lawrenceburg (Ind.) Gas Company.

5. Or, as it was told to the author, "we pay double to have the 'privilege' of being part of the System."

6. Columbus schools that used large amounts of natural gas were curtailed 40 percent for both the 1975 and 1976 winters, even before the unusual nature of winter 1977 was known. In contrast, Cincinnati schools were warned to expect a 28 percent cutback for large user schools in winter 1977. In actuality no curtailments occurred until December 30, 1976, and then only 20 percent of large user allocations.

7. At the time of this study, P.U.C.O. had regulatory control over all energy issues. Now Ohio's Department of Energy regulates certain fuels.

8. Paul Joskow, "Inflation and Environmental Concern: Structural Change in the Process of Utility Price Regulation," *Journal of Law and Economics* 17 (1974), 301-307, 314-320.

9. Ibid., p. 317.

10. Although lack of uniformity reveals at least as much about the style of the utility as the P.U.C.O. For example, the utility must present a particular desire before the commission will act. Columbia Gas of Ohio is much more an "active initiator" than CG and E. This helps explain why Columbia Gas of Ohio had a formal curtailment plan in 1972 and why CG and E filed in 1975.

11. All users are classified either industrial or domestic. As we will see, type of use classification becomes very important in determining fuel availability.

12. The discriminating reader will note the potential of a school district to use a "creative accounting" of base allocation in determining actual energy consumption. For example, if a large user could be converted to another heating fuel the base allocation amount could be used elsewhere.

13. Obviously, schools use natural gas for other purposes than just heating, so there is some usage in all twelve months.

14. "Broadened base" means that rather than have industries carry the burden to 100 percent, the limit was set at 40 percent, then small users (industrial) and commercial users (such as schools) were curtailed up to 40 percent.

15. "Carryover" is an important concept, for the schools can purchase summer (nonheating) surplus and it will not count against base allocation curtailments. For example, in the winter of 1975 Columbia Gas of Ohio had a large surplus of gas which it sold to Columbus schools at the same time it imposed a 40 percent *heating* season allocation curtailment. This "extra" supply became known as "crazy gas."

16. Actual comparison will concern the CG and E plan filed with P.U.C.O. on June 20, 1975, in relation to the *modified* Columbia Gas of Ohio, Inc., curtailment plan filed with P.U.C.O. July 25, 1975. Both plans were approved by P.U.C.O. on October 31, 1975. See *Interim Order*, P.U.C.O., no. 75-568-GA-AGC.

17. Columbus schools had a unique situation where forty-five large user facilities were also part of a total 152 facilities which used natural gas at the time of this study.

18. "Self Help Guidelines," P.U.C.O. case no. 73-761-Y, March 1976.

19. This stipulation was ignored by Columbus schools during the actual winter 1977 crisis.

20. Self-help to be on a curtailment schedule *below* residential user which, along with human needs, is lower than all industrial and commercial classifications. *Interim Report*, P.U.C.O., October 31, 1975.

21. The customer was responsible for all costs of production, development, and delivery. The average cost for drilling a 4,000-foot well was $88,000. The rates for self-help gas were two times as much as normal rates.

22. At the time of this study, federal price controls of interstate gas at well head were fifty-two cents per MCF for "old" gas and $1.42 per MCF for "new" gas (tapped after regulations established twenty-four years ago).

23. Repeated attempts by the project team to verify the policy relations between Columbia Gas of Ohio, Inc., and Columbia Gas Transmission Company concerning distribution met with failure. Consequently this section is based upon indirect inferences of the collected data by the author.

24. P.U.C.O., *Interim Report*, October 31, 1975.

25. Columbus and other school systems in Ohio made a special effort to be included in the exempt category but were denied. Instead, P.U.C.O. created a special school category that put large user schools in a third stage of curtailment up to 30 percent. Significantly, P.U.C.O. also specified that the *last* three groups to be curtailed are, in order, the remaining 70 percent school supplies, self-help gas and residents, or those in the human needs category. P.U.C.O. *Interim Order*, March 16, 1977.

26. In January 1974, SDE issued "Guidelines for Closing Schools Due to Lack of Fuel" and "Guidelines for the Conservation of Energy in Ohio Schools." These two booklets were distributed to all Ohio school districts. Later, in August 1974, an agreement was reached between SDE and Battelle Memorial Institute to produce energy conservation materials for teachers.

27. As a result of the Xenia tornado crisis of 1974 the SDE developed extensive, detailed plans for the mothballing of school facilities.

28. *Minutes*, Committee of the Whole, Columbus Public Schools, January 31, 1977.

29. "Energy Conservation Checklist," Plant Operations, Cincinnati Public Schools, undated.

30. Retrofitting is a term used to describe renovation and refurbishing of existing structures to become more energy efficient.

31. Quotation from Cincinnati administrator in plant operations, January 22, 1977.

32. *Minutes*, Committee of the Whole, Columbus Public Schools, January 31, 1977.

4

The Environmental Context

The last major variable affecting both interorganizational and intraorganizational variations in decision-making is the general policy environment in which the schools operate. To add some meaning to the general classification "large city school systems in an urban, conservative state," the policy environment for school governance will be divided into the board of education, the local community, municipal agencies, and state-wide agencies. However, some general information about the cities is helpful to set the stage for later comparisons.

General

Ohio is often characterized as a northern state and, as we have seen, the weather in Cincinnati and Columbus is approximately the same. However, inhabitants of the two cities are more likely to label themselves midwestern or even southern and tend to think of Ohio cities such as Cleveland or Toledo as being in "the north." Consequently, neither Columbus nor Cincinnati expected the large amounts of snow or continuous subzero temperatures which might have been a more normal occurrence in cities located in the "true" north.

Second, although Cincinnati and Columbus cities are located in metropolitan areas of nearly a million persons, the topography of the two areas is different. Cincinnati is built on "seven hills" which form the terrain on the banks of the Ohio River, while Columbus is located on the flat plateau in the middle of the state. During winter 1977 the terrain directly affected pupil transportation concerns. On a broader scale, the terrain affects the patterns of residence for the citizens. About half of the county residents live within the city limits of Cincinnati, compared to approximately two-thirds of the county residents in the Columbus metropolitan area.[1]

Cincinnati is a "poorer" city than Columbus in terms of overall family income (median), number of families with school-aged children, and poverty-level incomes and tangible personal property tax values.[2]

Most of the citizens in both cities are born in Ohio and are English-speaking.[3] The cities differ in the percents of black Americans and the mobility patterns of city residents. In the Cincinnati schools 53 percent of the children are black (1976 figures) and the mobility of students during a school year is 35 percent. This compares to 34 percent black students in Columbus schools, with a mobility of 14 percent.

From an educational perspective, a larger number of Columbus residents were engaged in some form of schooling activity (nursery through college) than their Cincinnati counterparts.[4] A subsection of this statistic is the difference between the cities in terms of numbers of school-aged children going to parochial or private schools. In 1970, approximately 25 percent of all school-aged Cincinnati children did not attend public schools, compared to 11 percent of the Columbus children.[5]

As will be discussed later in terms of characteristics of the school systems themselves, very few of the gross environmental characteristics can be directly attributed to interorganizational or intraorganizational responses to crisis by the school systems under study. The importance of this conclusion seems to be found in the contrast to the way the same information is incorporated into many planning efforts. For example, a crisis in school-community relationships would trigger interest in mobility patterns, racial characteristics, or geographic locations. In energy crises, we are more interested in other types of variables to plan or explain particular decisions made.

We now turn to specific governmental arrangements in the environment which may contribute to variation of decision response.

Boards of Education

In terms of formal authority, the seven-member Columbus Board of Education governs a city school system one-third larger in pupil enrollment than their Cincinnati board counterparts.[6] However, the formal authority and normal relation to public school governance have little to do with the actual policy relationship of board to the school system during the time of this study. A major conclusion of this study was the lack of real governance and direction exhibited by either board of education during the winter 1977 crisis.[7] In actual decision-making, crisis response was an administrative matter and the board's role was as part of the "external environment." Although retaining the formal authority to decide the fate of Cincinnati and Columbus schools during the emergency, neither board was inclined to act independently of directions given by the central administration to establish a crisis response. In fact, only one board member in either city asked informed questions about the nature of the 1977 winter and energy shortages or expressed public skepticism about the administration's preferences for action. While it is true in a technical sense that the Cincinnati board decided to authorize the host-guest arrangement and the Columbus board decided to implement "School Without Schools," the actual dynamics of choice suggest a "nondecision."[8] While the boards could have decided other policy options, the choices would have looked irrational in a situation already "wild." The central administration held whatever technical and political information was available concerning this type of crisis. The board had no choice but to go along with their "suggestions" to appear to make an informed decision. In winter 1977, the boards of education were true "agencies of legitimization"[9] concerning crucial decisions about crisis response.

The importance of the policy role forced upon each board during winter 1977 is emphasized by the fact that both boards often operate in a crisis context and with some skepticism of the central administration. Each school system had been under legal challenge for several years, facing charges of deliberate racial segregation. The "ifs and hows" of achieving desegregated school conditions had affected board member candidacy and selection since the early 1970s. Individuals and slates of candidates ran on "liberal" or "conservative" platforms and both school systems have had "split, nonconsensus" boards of education for some time. Although the Cincinnati and Columbus boards were used to deciding in the crisis-prone issue context of race (as well as poor finances, teacher strikes, and other normal big-city crises), the 1977 winter crisis immobilized their proactive judgments.

The passive role of the boards during winter 1977 gains further importance when the general skepticism of the central administration and professional expertise is considered. Although neither board was hostile to the superintendent or major central office administrative incumbents in winter 1977, both school boards had long records of sharply questioning professional judgments and policy options presented by the administration on a wide variety of educational matters. However, the unexpected severity of the 1977 winter conditions, the lack of technical knowledge or feelings of expertise among board members and the lack of time were perceived as the major reasons why the board should take a passive or indirect decision role. Several Cincinnati and Columbus board members even suggested that cold weather and energy shortages were not educational issues but "problems of administrative implementation." A hindsight perspective of the fundamental decisions made during winter 1977 may give the impression that the boards negated their leadership responsibility. However, during the actual throes of uncertainty and crisis activity, it seemed a logical policy stance to most board incumbents.

Municipal Agencies and the Local Community

One of the major differences between the Columbus and Cincinnati stories of crisis response to winter 1977 was the policy role of the municipal government and local community. Although there was some help and coordination, the Cincinnati schools faced the crisis of winter 1977 essentially "on their own." That judgment is substantiated when Cincinnati is compared to Columbus, where the support of the city was pervasive and an integral part of major crisis response activities.

Both cities seem similar under the conventional "community power structure" type of analysis which would determine influence and sources of potential help or hindrance to the schools. The Columbus power structure is characterized by the particular influences of a local radio and television conglomerate, department-store chain, certain banks, and (depending on whose interpretation) Ohio State University. Cincinnati power is concentrated in the banks, industries such as food processing, heavy machinery, trucking, and Proctor and Gamble. In the past, both power structures have offered specific help and resources to the city schools and demonstrated their essential commitment to the belief that the public schools are vehicles to maintaining a good community. However, in general, Cincinnati industries represent a political culture more *laissez-faire* about the role of schools and government than their Columbus counterparts. Throughout the turmoil of the late 1960s and early 1970s, the Columbus power structure played a persistent and overtly public role in school matters. The Cincinnati activities of support were more sporadic and covert during the same time period. In winter 1977 the Columbus community rallied to the School Without Schools venture with a significant influx of resources. Several Columbus school officials commented that the donations of television and radio time, bus services, and numerous facilities were what made School Without Schools possible.

In contrasting the relation of municipal governments to the two school systems, the role of mayor becomes important. Both cities have a mayor-city council form of government. Both school systems are fiscally independent of their municipal government but there are numerous "shared services" which blur school and government boundaries. In normal times, the city government and mayor have little to do with ongoing school policy matters. However, during the winter of 1977, the Columbus mayor became a key figure in the School Without Schools effort while his counterpart in Cincinnati was not extensively involved in school adaptation efforts. Obviously, the type of adaptation effort attempted by both school systems mandated different needs and expectations upon the policy roles of the city government and mayor's office. Although it borders on a chicken or egg type of distinction, this study suggests that wholesale change efforts by the schools during an energy crisis are dependent upon the receptivity of the municipal government. Anything less than enthusiastic and committed support by the local mayor during the crisis period of winter 1977 may well have placed School Without Schools in the "impractical" or "not plausible" category of policy options. It may well be this support, rather than time and money, that was the most significant difference between the two cities and their school systems during winter 1977.

State Agencies

Perhaps the major environmental differences between the two school systems under study was the location of Columbus schools in the state capital. Columbus schools were publicly acknowledged by the governor and legislature as the "light-house" system for the state in adapting to the 1977 winter crisis. Columbus administrators had worked much more closely with ongoing State Department of Education efforts to alleviate energy concerns for schools than did their Cincinnati counterparts. As noted in chapter 2, the specific proposal of the Columbus superintendent of schools was ultimately translated into emergency legislation for school compensation. As we will see, his proposal also provided interpretation standards for SDE judgments of transportation compensation.

In contrast, Cincinnati schools had little direct relationship with the governor's office, legislature, or SDE concerning the 1977 winter crisis. They, like most other school districts in Ohio, had to wait for directions from "on high" to structure their emergency planning. The Cincinnati response to this relationship was to ignore state-level agencies as much as possible and to deal with winter 1977 as a local concern.

Conclusions

In a very real sense, the relationship of both the school systems to the various agencies within their policy environments explains the type of crisis response attempted. Two major conclusions can be made about the policy environments of the Cincinnati and Columbus school systems. First, crisis adaptation was a professional educator and technician effort. The board of education in each system acted as an "agency of legitimization" for decisions reached by the administrative structure. This reality differentiates energy types of crisis from social-oriented crisis (for example, race relations or pupil achievement) where boards of education play an active, major role.

The second major conclusion is that both school systems decided, in part, upon the critical issue of crisis adaptation by major reorganization versus refinement of existing normal operations based upon a calculation of potential external support by local and state governmental agencies. Cincinnati schools, located in the southern part of the state with a municipal government preoccupied with a *laissez-faire* attitude toward educational concerns, chose an "insider, business as usual" response strategy. Without the guarantees of external resources or critical political coalitions with key agencies, the options of radical reform or new types of school organization were unfeasible.

On the other hand, the Columbus schools decided to initiate School Without Schools on the assurances of support from the external environment. As we will see in future discussions, the actual support proved to be substantial.

To this point we have discussed the broad environmental variables which could affect intra- and interorganizational variations in school system decision response. We now turn to the school systems themselves.

Notes

1. In 1970 Hamilton County (which surrounds Cincinnati) had 923,205 residents while the number of residents within the Cincinnati school jurisdiction was 484,597. Franklin County (which incorporates the Columbus schools) had 833,249 residents in 1970, 511,129 of whom lived within the Columbus school jurisdiction boundaries.

2. All information cited in this section elicited from National Center Educational Statistics, "Social and Economic Characteristics of School Districts: April 1970," pp. 838-856, 1006-1024; or the International City Management Association, *The Municipal Yearbook* (1976, Volume 43, Washington, D.C., Cities over 10,000: 1975).

3. Cincinnati has a larger German population and more immigrants from Appalachian areas.

4. In 1970 over 159,000 Columbus residents were engaged in educational activities, compared to 137,000 Cincinnati citizens.

5. From a population of 122,000 Columbus school-aged children, 15,000 attended parochial or private schools compared to 27,000 of the 115,000 Cincinnati school-aged children (statistics rounded to nearest thousand).

6. The 1975-76 average daily membership of Cincinnati public schools was 66,187 compared to Columbus ADM of 93,176. Figures from Ohio Public Expenditure Council Report 23-18, 1976.

7. Special thanks is given to Carol Smith and Paula Saunders for their study of this particular matter.

8. "Nondecisions" are a deliberate form of choice where events are allowed to structure their own outcome. A famous example of this process was President Coolidge's "calculated inactivity."

9. The term was first coined by Norman Kerr, "The School Board as an Agency of Legitimization," *Sociology of Education* 38(1964), 34-59.

5

Central Office Arrangements

The extent to which Cincinnati and Columbus public schools varied in crisis response to winter 1977 is most visible from an organizational perspective. At the central office level of internal organization, the difference in response becomes two separate stories of administrative operation. Cincinnati central office operated, essentially, under regular arrangements with several individuals taking on new or expanded administrative responsibilities. Columbus central office operated under new administrative structure during the entire emergency period that School Without Schools was in effect. The extent of difference in organizational response is even more pronounced in light of statistics which compare the normal characteristics of the two school systems.

On paper, there are few pieces of information which could explain why the two systems differed so radically in crisis response. Columbus public schools is the larger system in terms of average student enrollment, numbers of elementary, junior high/middle school and senior high buildings, and numbers of teaching personnel. In 1975-76 Columbus schools had an average daily membership of 93,178, compared to Cincinnati's 66,187. Nonvocational and nonspecial educational students were housed in 156 Columbus facilities, compared to 93 Cincinnati local school centers. At the time of this study, Columbus had sixteen senior high shools (grades 10-12), twenty-six junior highs (grades 7-9) and seventy-one elementary schools. In 1976, there were 4,689 Columbus classroom teachers and 2,916 Cincinnati classroom teachers.

Financially, Cincinnati students fared somewhat better than their Columbus counterparts. The school operating revenue per pupil based upon total property taxes (1976 calendar year) was $777 for Cincinnati students, compared to $645 for Columbus students (property tax as percent of total revenue was 65 percent for Cincinnati and 60 percent for Columbus). In 1975-76 total costs per pupil for current expenses were $1,440 in Cincinnati and $1,342 in Columbus. This compared with a state-wide average of $1,172 and a $1,101 average for the ten largest cities in Ohio.

Statistics related to centralized governance also fail to explain the dramatic variation in crisis response during winter 1977. The data do show, however, that the normal central office arrangements did have different characteristics. In 1976, Cincinnati had 4.6 percent of total cost per pupil for current expenses in the general control category (approximately $66 per pupil), compared to 2.6 percent of total Columbus per pupil costs for general control ($35). At the time of this study, the state-wide average for general control was $45 per pupil while the average for the ten largest Ohio cities was $47.[1]

The breakdown in administrative titles also reveals different emphases upon central governance in the two school systems. Although both school systems had a single superintendent of schools and single deputy/associate superintendent of schools in 1976,[2] Cincinnati had four "assistant superintendents," compared to nine such adminstrators in Columbus. Cincinnati had one finance/business administrator compared to six such personnel in Columbus. On the other hand, Cincinnati had nineteen staff personnel administrators, compared to six in Columbus. Both systems had numerous subject area supervisors (forty-three in Cincinnati, fifty-eight in Columbus) although Cincinnati had many more individuals listed as "other advisors" (seventy-seven in Cincinnati compared to twenty-one in Columbus).

Comparison of the structural arrangements for the two school systems also reveals different emphases but not specific clauses to interorganizational variation in crisis response to winter 1977. Figure 5-1 presents the structural organization of the Cincinnati central office at the time of this study.

In contrast to the normal Columbus arrangement (presented later), Cincinnati's structural organization reflected both functional differentiation (human resources, curriculum and instruction, research and development, support) and regional decentralization (elementary schools into three geographic regions and junior and senior highs into two). Columbus schools did not have an intermediate administrative tier for select regions, and it is interesting to note such a tier was created[3] for the emergency adaptation to winter 1977.

Figure 5-2 presents the Columbus central office structural governance arrangement at the time of the study.

The discerning reader will note the specific reference to energy management under the functions of the assistant superintendent for management services. Although there was some disagreement among respondents as to whether this was a formal responsibility prior to winter 1977, the fact that an Energy Crisis Committee existed since 1975 is commonly recognized. This committee was chaired by an assistant superintendent and had direct liaison with the Columbus Superintendent of Schools. The committee further considered energy consumption data generated from internal audits on a regular basis and was responsible for coordinating efforts which created the *School Without Schools Handbook*. Because of these activities, the classification energy management was included as a regular, ongoing function of the Columbus central office.

In summary, the normal central office arrangements of the two school systems do not, in themselves, explain variation in decision response during winter 1977. The school systems were somewhat different in size, governmental emphases, and particular role expectations for administrators. Yet, the general inference would probably be that Cincinnati and Columbus are more alike in resembling the conventional characteristics of big-city school systems[4] and, thus, would probably operate in much the same fashion.

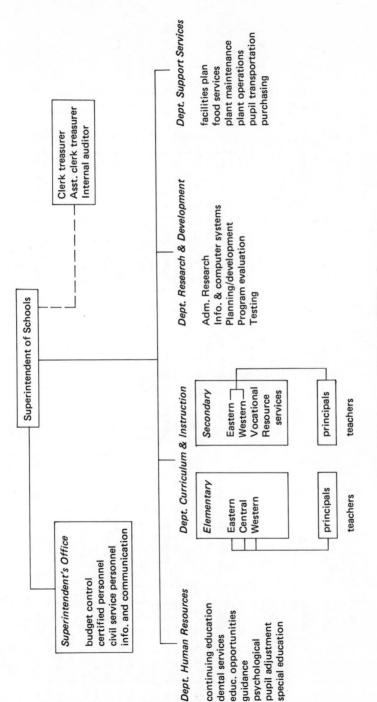

Figure 5-1. Cincinnati Central Office Governance

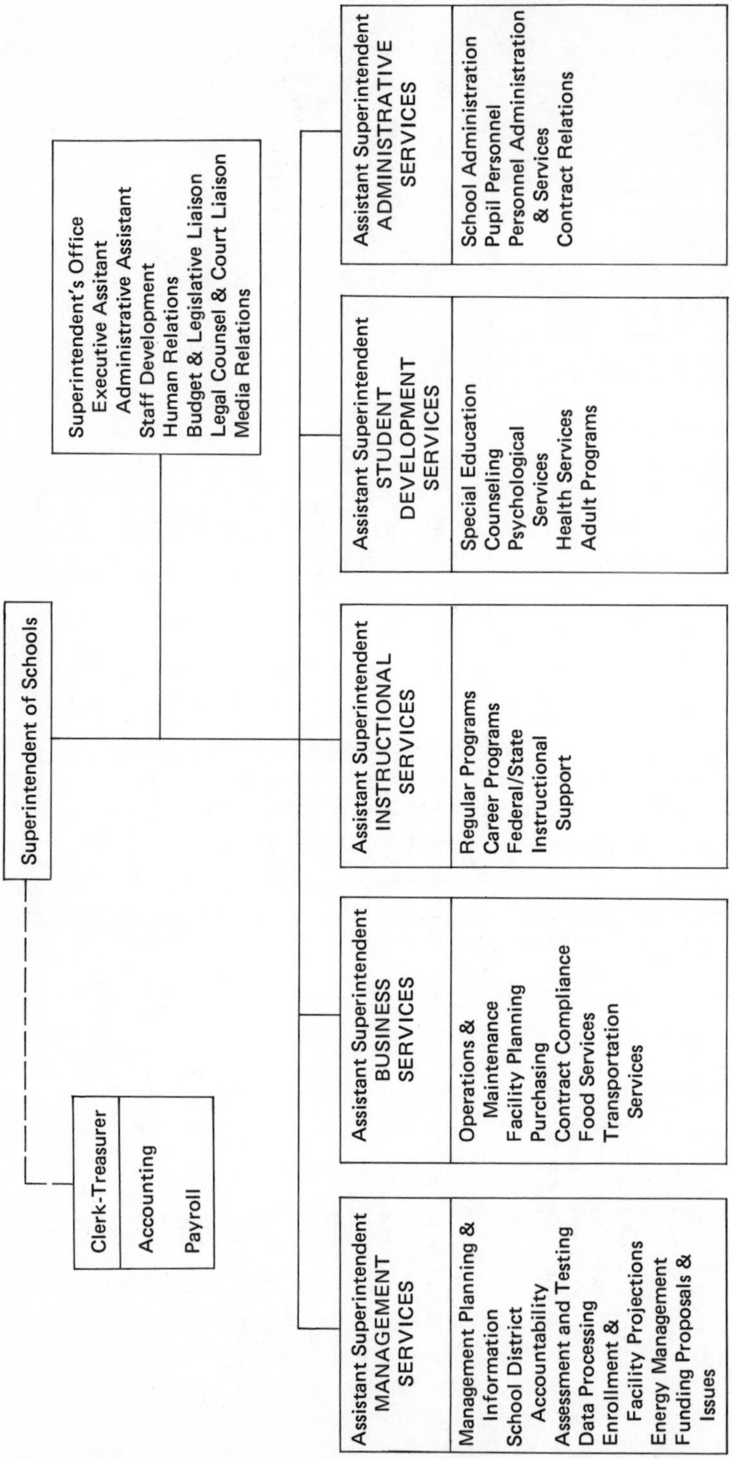

Superintendent's Office
Executive Assitant
Administrative Assistant
Staff Development
Human Relations
Budget & Legislative Liaison
Legal Counsel & Court Liaison
Media Relations

Superintendent of Schools

Clerk-Treasurer
Accounting
Payroll

Assistant Superintendent MANAGEMENT SERVICES
Management Planning & Information
School District Accountability
Assessment and Testing
Data Processing
Enrollment & Facility Projections
Energy Management
Funding Proposals & Issues

Assistant Superintendent BUSINESS SERVICES
Operations & Maintenance
Facility Planning
Purchasing
Contract Compliance
Food Services
Transportation Services

Assistant Superintendent INSTRUCTIONAL SERVICES
Regular Programs
Career Programs
Federal/State
Instructional Support

Assistant Superintendent STUDENT DEVELOPMENT SERVICES
Special Education
Counseling
Psychological Services
Health Services
Adult Programs

Assistant Superintendent ADMINISTRATIVE SERVICES
School Administration
Pupil Personnel
Personnel Administration & Services
Contract Relations

Figure 5-2. Columbus Central Office Governance

Like the normal indicators of school environment discussed in chapter 4, the conventional descriptors of administrative organization do not tell us much about crisis response. This has important, practical implicatons for planning which will be discussed later. For now, this conclusion means we must look to other data to explain interorganizational variations.

Columbus

The Columbus central office arrangements during winter 1977 reflected the total organization commitment to an entirely new form of operation of the public schools. The emergency arrangement of the central office can be described in two phases; events prior to the implementation of School Without Schools and actual operations during the month of School Without Schools.

At the onset of the 1977 winter crisis (that is, late December 1976, early January 1977) but prior to implementation of School Without Schools, the Columbus central office attempted to operate normally, with certain administrators taking on special roles. Four such roles stand out; the superintendent of schools and his staff, the administrator in charge of coordinating the ongoing Energy Crisis Committee, the administrative effort to secure additional emergency supplies of natural gas (called self-help gas), and the administrative coordination with teaching and noncertified personnel organizations.

The Columbus Superintendent of Schools during winter 1977[5] was a nationally known public figure with a well-established reputation of strong influence in state and national professional circles. The superintendent played a major personal role in the initial coordination, publicizing, and securing of external resources to undertake School Without Schools. As early as January 1975, the superintendent charged the Energy Crisis Committee with the following responsibilities:

a. To review our present sources of fuel consumption and supply.
b. To review the current heating, ventilating and lighting practices.
c. To consider whether inservice training for teachers, principals and classified personnel can contribute to fuel savings.
d. To establish a system of tentative priorities for operating the schools in the event sufficient fuel is not available.
e. To consider communication with parents, the news media and others to insure cooperation and understanding.

Thus, the Columbus schools began a systematic, anticipatory planning effort two years before the 1977 crisis at the insistence of the chief school officer.

As noted in the earlier chapter on the crisis chronology, the Columbus Superintendent of Schools played a major role in influencing state legislators, State Department of Education personnel, and members of the governor's staff in their selection of appropriate emergency adaptation measures. The personal impact of the Columbus superintendent is particularly apparent in two pieces of emergency legislation passed during winter 1977. Senate Bill 51 (February 2,

1977) allowed schools to be reimbursed by state aid for up to fifteen "emergency" days. House Bill 176 (February 17, 1977) eliminated a 120-day waiting period before school districts could receive Title XX (public welfare) funds to conduct field trips and authorized the expenditure of such title funds for adaptation efforts during the 1977 winter emergency.

Both legislative efforts contributed significant external resources to the implementation of the Columbus School Without Schools effort. In addition, the Columbus superintendent is identified as being personally responsible for the close liaison among the public schools, municipal government, and critical agencies in the community. For example, the superintendent helped to facilitate the donation of certain bus services and use of municipal buildings from the mayor's office; he persuaded the College of Education of Ohio State University to offer special learning opportunities and the local television and radio stations to contribute significant time and effort to emergency school activities.[6]

Finally, the superintendent played a strong personal role in alleviating possible misunderstandings among contractual personnel within the Columbus school system. For example, classroom teacher federation personnel were part of the crucial decision structure for both the planning and implementation of School Without Schools.

A second administrative role of special responsibility prior to the actual School Without Schools effort was the coordination of the Energy Crisis Committee. The committee acted as the major organization vehicle in keeping the Board of Education and members of the school system informed of possible emergency plans for action. The composition[7] of the committee made it particularly well suited to consider emergency plans which would involve large amounts of participation among various constituents within the school system. It was this committee that did much of the feasibility considerations which resulted, ultimately, in the *Handbook* document and the administrative arrangements during School Without Schools.

The *Handbook* and efforts to construct such a document deserve a special mention in relation to pre-School Without Schools adaptation efforts. Committee members and other administrative and teaching personnel of the school system began to assemble the *Handbook* on January 21, 1977. By February 1, a document of over 200 pages describing the "who, how, when, where, and whys" of the emergency adaptation labeled School Without Schools was distributed to personnel at all local school centers.[8] The administrative coordination necessary to accomplish such an effort in so short a time speaks for itself.[9]

A third special administrative role involved school efforts to secure additional supplies of emergency natural gas. The supplies, called self-help gas, were being sought by an external, nonprofit group called Gas, Inc., during the month of January 1977. It is difficult to recreate the uncertainty and frantic activity of that time so that the role of administrative coordination can be fully appreciated. As we will see more fully in subsequent discussions, the normal dynamics by which natural gas is secured are highly technical and involve many policy actors foreign to most educators. Under emergency conditions, the situation in January 1977 resembled a "poker game gone wild." The Columbus schools were most fortunate in having several administrators with technical backgrounds and experience to interpret procurement efforts to their professional colleagues.[10]

The final special role prior to School Without Schools involved the coordination of the school system's planning with various contractual personnel. The continuous involvement of teacher federation representatives in all central office thinking was widely cited as the major reason School Without Schools was accomplished. Like many big-city school systems, the history of relationships between the central office administration and teacher federation was somewhat marred by conflict and hostility. Only strong personal effort[11] and commitment to share in all emergency planning allowed the critical contract modifications and other activities necessary to secure the help of teachers to occur.[12]

General Emergency Operations

During the month of February 1977 (as School Without Schools was implemented) the Columbus central office operated under an emergency format spelled out in detail by the *Handbook*. A special organization was created to provide curricular and instructional options during the emergency. The "regular program" was divided into four administrative arrangements: academic humanities, elementary programs, science and mathematics, physical education and health. A second central office program coordination effort grouped continuing education, adult education, practical education (for example, industrial arts), and safety education.[13]

Along with the general reorganization of the central office during the emergency, Columbus schools maintained a continuous monitoring unit, labeled the Emergency Operations Center.[14] The center conducted a number of major operations, including the provision of a "hotline"/rumor control function, monitoring pupil attendance and transportation needs from local schools (especially difficult tasks under the decentralized School Without Schools plan), and facilitating field trips. To appreciate the extent of effort by the center consider that in the first week of School Without Schools 83 percent of all Columbus schools called the central office to arrange for outside programs. This meant the anticipated involvement of more than 47,000 children in some field trip activity. Tours included such facilities as metropolitan zoos and parks, fire and police stations, the Ohio legislature, Columbus libraries, local business establishments for recreation (used for alternate physical education activities), cultural organizations (such as the Gallery of Fine Arts), the U.S. Post Office, local newspapers, county courthouse, and Ohio State University.[15]

Special Emergency Operations

The final area of central office reorganization for the emergency was in the specialized functions of plant maintenance and security, food services, athletics, and radio/television programming. Each of these functions operated virtually independent from general administrative coordination and, as such, they present separate stories of emergency adaptation efforts. Although each function will be discussed more fully in subsequent chapters, several illustrations serve to hint at the extensiveness of central office coordination.

February is the height of basketball season, when league championships are decided and individual teams make bids for state championships. Columbus is a hotbed of interest in interscholastic athletics, and it was decided early on that team sports would continue if at all possible. The extent to which the energy crisis added additonal administrative concern and effort to carry out athletics is captured in the following statement.

> Due to the energy crisis, a number of adjustments have been made in our senior high school boys' and girls' basketball programs. We will continue to have our games and to have practices. However, schools that are closed due to using natural gas for fuel will have to play all games and conduct all practices at a school site that is open due to a source of fuel other than natural gas. For both the boys' and girls' basketball we will remain with the *dates* that are now on our schedules but some floors will be reversed or in the case of two gas burning schools playing they will be assigned to a neutral floor. . . .

> At gas burning schools coaches should take home and away uniforms, warm-ups, balls, scorebooks, medicine kits, etc. home. You are not to enter your building each time you have a practice or a game for these items. Have your players take all practice and game gear home as they are not to enter your building before each practice and game. . . .

> When two schools have their game assigned to a neutral floor, the original home school faculty manager will administer the game at the neutral site, e.g. School A vs. School B at Site C. School B is the original home school—so the School B faculty manager will administer the game at site C, take your ticket seller, ticket taker, police, etc. to Site C. The site C faculty manager will be on duty at site C, even if his team is playing away, to assist the School B faculty manager in where to sell and take tickets, where to station police, where locker rooms are, to have bleachers out, to have scoreboard controls ready, to have building open and closed, etc. The School B faculty manager should call the site C faculty manager in advance of game to determine what personnel will be needed to administer the game at site C.[16]

Although some administrative confusion resulted, the athletics program continued throughout the 1977 crisis with a minimum of disruption.[17]

A second example of modification of a specialized service during the crisis is in the food services area. This is an $8 million enterprise within the Columbus schools, and a researchers notes capture the emergency adjustment made during School Without Schools.

> Radical changes in procedure characterized the food services effort during the "School Without Schools" period. Assignment and inservice training were modified. Most food services people are paid regular salaries for contracted hours (usually 4) and then receive overtime for frequently extended hours (the first 2 at regular pay). Between February 7 and 25, overtime was entirely eliminated, and workers from the 150 closed schools were lent to all of the functioning ones for assistance—in food service and other duties. The Food Production Center prepared additional cold lunches for classes meeting in non-school locations and regular meals for thirty community centers. In other words, any child in Columbus who wanted his free, partial payment, or pay lunch could get it on any day. Mr. Hartman credits his central kitchen operations, newly installed telephones, and computers for the success of this massive effort. There were more personnel than necessary at some locations but no one worried much about it.[18]

In summary, the Columbus central office arrangements to respond to winter 1977 must be understood in two phases. Prior to School Without Schools, there were special administrative roles necessary to consider the feasibility of massive emergency reorganization. These roles dealt with securing of external resources and establishing critical internal understandings among various school system constituents. Once the emergency plan was actually implemented, a second phase of central office arrangements was necessary. This phase involved general academic reorganization, provision of emergency operations coordination, and the semiautonomous operation of select specialized services. The sum effect of the two phases warrants the conclusion that Columbus schools totally revamped existing central office arrangements to cope with the 1977 winter. We now turn to quite a different story of crisis response at the central office level.

Cincinnati

In contrast to Columbus, the Cincinnati central office maintained normal central office arrangements throughout winter 1977. Emergency adaptation was confined to special activities undertaken by select administrators with little structural modification. For example, there were few administrative roles created especially for the winter emergency and there was no modification of the existing master contract with the teaching personnel. The central level crisis response of Cincinnati schools is more aptly discussed as "maintaining normalcy in trying times" than reorganizing to cope with extreme conditions. Consequently, crisis response of the school system was on a day-to-day assessment of inclement weather conditions. Further, all public announcements were made by the superintendent of schools as head of the formal organization.

The Cincinnati superintendent operated with the advice of his cabinet as a normal way to make major decisions.[19] The following memo from the cabinet outlines their perception of how the superintendent should operate during a winter emergency;

> The committee agreed that I should write you this memo identifying the need for a clear understanding about who will assume what responsibility for communications. Therefore, we are suggesting that you make immediate decisions based on alternatives regarding the following points.
>
> 1. We assume you will make the final decision on whether to close schools or not. In conjuction with that, you should decide the persons with whom you will consult in order to make that decision. In either event, the decision should be made no later than 5:00 a.m. of the day schools are to be closed.
>
> 2. The committee recommends that the Transportation Coordinator assume responsibility for calling the superintendent directly when the weather becomes inclement overnight. This call will take place at approximately 5:00 a.m. Therefore, all consultation should be completed in time to allow the announcement to be made beginning with the 6:00 a.m. news broadcast. The Transportation Coordinator will be prepared to share with the Superintendent the present weather conditions, latest weather forecast, highway maintenance report, and the bus contractors report.
>
> 3. The Transportation Coordinator will then be responsible for giving the media the appropriate message based on the Superintendent's decision.
>
> 4. No other Cabinet or staff member should call the Transportation Coordinator unless directed to do so by the Superintendent. This strict communication arrangement will help avoid misinterpretations.
>
> 5. When appropriate, the Superintendent should communicate with Cabinet Members regarding inclement weather decisions.
>
> 6. Cabinet Members are expected to review the written policy, procedures and announcements with the staff under their respective supervision.
>
> 7. All staff should be officially informed that each person is responsible for contacting his or her supervisor if there is any doubt about reporting to work.[20]

It is important to remember the decision context for Cincinnati schools during the first month of crisis in winter 1977. Unlike Columbus, heating fuel seemed less a problem than pupil transportation during January. The crux of emergency decision making was (a) how to gather critical transportation and weather information to make a judgment to operate the schools and (b) how to communicate such a decision to school personnel and the public.

The following directive outlines how the emergency process of how central office decision were made.

General Rule

The superintendent is empowered to close the district schools, delay the opening, or to dismiss them early in the event of hazardous weather which threatens the safety of students. Such action is never to be taken lightly, for public education is one of the principal functions of the community and should be maintained at a normal level except in extreme circumstances. While it may be prudent, under certain circumstances, to excuse students from attending school, to delay the opening hour, or to dismiss students early, the administration has the responsibility to see that as much of the administrative, supervisory, and operational activity is continued as may be possible.

In making the decision to close schools, either the superintendent or his designee shall consider many factors, including the following principal ones relating to the fundamental concern for the safety and health of children:

A. Weather conditions, both existing and predicted;
B. Driving and traffic conditions affecting public and private transportation facilities;
C. Continuance or discontinuance of the operations of business, commercial, and professional people in the city.

Facts are assembled from the appropriate agencies and organizations, for example, the Highway Department, Police Department, Weather Bureau, and transportation companies.

Following the decision, communications will begin for the total notification of the students and staff. Either the superintendent or his designee shall notify the public media. Employees should listen to broadcasts beginning at 6:00 a.m. Any employee who is doubtful about reporting should contact his/her immediate supervisor.

Delayed School Plan

When it seems likely that weather and/or street conditions will improve later in the morning, a "delayed school opening" announcement may be made to the public. Employees shall make an effort to report to their assignment at the regular starting time.

"A" Schedule (One Hour Delay in All School Starting Times) All schools will begin one hour later than normal starting times and dismiss at regular time.

"B" Schedule (Two Hour Delay in All School Starting Times) All schools will begin two hours later than normal starting times and dismiss at regular time. No A.M. Kindergarten and P.M. Pre-School will be held as scheduled.[21]

Besides the superintendent, the person most involved in the critical day-to-day decision-making was the transportation coordinator.[22] This person was responsible for finding out whether the municipal buses and private bus/taxi operators would be working on a particular school day. As the January weather worsened, the role of transportation coordinator became increasingly untenable. Various contracted agencies responsible for bringing children to school operated under varying definitions of "hazardous" conditions. At first, the judgment of "hazard" had seemed to rest upon factors such as snow accumulated, whether roads were icy, and other weather data. As January progressed various transportation operators began to act on perceived risk to insurance for liability and the length of delays to accomplish the transportation task (sometimes up to two hours late). The Cincinnati school transportation coordinator often had to transmit his recommendations for closing, delayed opening, or regular opening on sketchy and ambiguous information. This problem was never completely resolved during winter 1977 operations but it was one of the realities which caused Cincinati to undertake further emergency modifications in central office arrangement.

The emphasis on the day-to-day crisis decision-making about school operation may have created the impression that there was no concern for the natural gas situation. This was not true. Administrators responsible for plant operations and maintenance had conducted systematic fuel consumption audits since 1975. An ad hoc committee established to share school-based information about fuel consumption and conservation efforts with industries and municipal agencies in the Cincinnati community was created in the fall of 1976.[23] However, all these activities were treated as temporary modifications of the routine arrangements.

As we have seen in the earlier chapter on chronology, the crisis for Cincinnati schools reached a peak toward the last week of January[24] and necessitated further central office rearrangements. A committee to design and coordinate the implementation of the host-guest pairing plan was the most visible emergency alteration. Part of the visibility was due to the committee's being chaired by an administrator of one of the junior-senior high school regional areas[25] rather than a central office member of the cabinet. This committee operated directly with the local schools and support services implementing the host-guest plan during February 1977.

Another emergency arrangement for February was the formation of a committee to utilize television for alternative instruction. A researcher's field notes capture the flavor of these emergency efforts;

In less than twenty-four hours, a schedule of television programs had been worked out. Arrangements were made to pull teachers to work on tapes. By Tuesday, two and a half days' worth of educational television programs had been put on tape. There was a problem with using WCET since all taping had to be done at night. As a result, public television was used rather than WCET. All teachers working on tapes did so voluntarily. Within the television design were plans for assignments which would be given on television and in the newspapers with the possibility of their being mailed in or returned to the schools every third day for the teacher to pick up; the students could also hold them until their return.[26]

A final emergency arrangement concerned the provision of food services to pupils involved in the host-guest exchange. Children being transported to the schools were missing regular lunch periods. The emergency efforts of a single food services administrator[27] are credited with solving this problem through the provision of box lunches.

In summary, the Cincinnati central office engaged in modified operations only when emergency conditions mandated such a change. Even then, all modification was based upon how to approximate regular conditions as much as possible. Like Columbus, those subunits forced to operate on an emergency basis (for example, the transportation coordinator, administration of the host-guest effort and food services) acted as semiautonomous units. Decisions made by these units during the crisis were not overridden by the larger central office bureaucracy.

Conclusions

Scrutiny of the raw data profiles and organizational charts of the Cincinnati and Columbus school systems gives little hint as to how the systems responded to winter crisis. Comparison of actual crisis activities shows one central office responding by total, planned reorganization and the other central office entering into emergency modifications with restraint and reluctance.

Both systems were alike in the phased implementation of emergency arrangements, although the phases were very different for the two school systems. The first phase in Columbus involved the preliminary assessments of internal arrangements and external resources necessary to undertake School Without Schools. The second phase was the creation of an elaborate document (the *Handbook*) and well thought out reorganization to implement the School Without Schools effort.

In Cincinnati, the first phase of emergency adaptation was attempting to assess weather and transportation data to make daily judgments about school opening. The second phase was to implement select emergency activities which were found necessary to keep schools operating at normal.

Both school systems were also alike in that the emergency arrangements made necessitated new roles for certain administrators. In Columbus, all roles were rearranged somewhat for School Without Schools. During the crisis, certain roles became the key decision points in central office functioning. Of particular note were the role of the superintendent of schools, administrators associated with efforts to secure natural gas and other fuels, and persons responsible for negotiations with contracted personnel. Certain specialized areas, such as food services, acted in virtual autonomy.

In Cincinnati, the role of transportation coordinator, the administrator for food services, and the operation of the special "host-guest" plan took on special significance. Personnel in these emergency roles enjoyed increased authority and responsibility *vis-à-vis* normal central office arrangements.

In the discussion of this chapter we have taken a system-wide, central office perspective of crisis adaptation. We now turn to a local school focus of the same phenomenon.

Notes

1. A major reason given for the spring of 1977 teacher strike in Cincinnati was release of a State Department of Education report purported to show Cincinnati administratively top heavy at a time teachers were being laid off jobs.

2. The numbers and titles of administrative personnel are intended to give a rough comparison of overall governance emphasis rather than a particular breakdown at some time in 1977 or today. In fact, both Cincinnati and Columbus, like most major school systems, are continuously modifying the particular composition and format of their administrative structure.

3. Although the tier looked very different in that it was composed of "clusters" of local school administrators rather than regional directors.

4. Conventional in the sense of standard textbook description of line/staff bureaucratic arrangements and functional responsibilities.

5. Dr. John Ellis in March 1977 became employed in the U.S. Office of Education.

6. The superintendent or his staff also made special coordinative efforts with the Roman Catholic schools, City Parks and Recreation, the Center for Science and Industry, and the Battelle Institute prior to and during the 1977 winter emergency.

7. The committee, chaired by an assistant superintendent, consisted of central office and local school administrators, teachers, board members, and technicians responsible for plant maintenance and operation.

8. Drafts of the *Handbook* were approved by the board along with School Without Schools on January 31, 1977. The handbooks were distributed to all principals at a local high school the following day.

9. Dr. Phil Fulton, Dr. Howard Merriman, and Mr. Edwin Tilton were most identified with this effort.

10. Of special note in this regard was Dr. Calvin Smith.

11. Particularly Superintendent Ellis and Dr. Charles Hall.

12. A major characteristic of School Without Schools was the extent of personal effort and sacrifice by teachers "above and beyond the call" of contractual duties.

13. Some of the central office emergency grouping was more fiction than real. For example, adult education operated uninterrupted and without modification throughout the emergency period.

14. Headed during the emergency by Mr. Don Davies.

15. As a further indication of how extensive the transportation coordination function was, in a fifteen-day period, 1,722 bus trips were scheduled and taken. In the week February 14-18, 36,676 students were involved. In the following week, 41,416 students participated (of the 96,000 total enrollment).

16. Memo to all principals, coaches, and mangers from Jane Walter and Don McCaulsky, February 1, 1977.

17. The major complaints were that practice and games were conducted in gyms with temperatures less than 50°, when games were played back to back, and that private transportation had to be secured.

18. Excerpted from report "The Personnel Function of the Columbus Schools," prepared by Carol Smith (mimeographed, 1978). Under normal conditions, Columbus elementary schools receive lunches prepackaged in three sections at a central location. Food services people at the building level simply collect money, and heat and distribute the food.

19. The Superintendent of Schools was Dr. James Jacobs. The cabinet consisted of the assistant superintendents in charge of four functions. See figure 5-1.

20. Internal memo, January 8, 1977, based upon an existing regulation for closing schools due to inclement weather dated January 14, 1976.

21. Memo to all school personnel, January 10, 1977.

22. Mr. Jerome Couzins.

23. Although the committee met prior to and during the winter 1977 crisis there were few decisions concerning major coordinative activities. Most discussion involved the trading of technical status reports about the effects of voluntary conservation efforts.

24. Notification by Cincinnati Gas and Electric that 20 percent curtailments of natural gas allocation would be much more.

25. Mr. Frank Fields of the western region of secondary schools. See figure 5-1. There was also a plan to use the elementary central region administrator to coordinate teacher utilization if all schools closed but it was not implemented.

26. Report prepared by Paula Saunders. The actual use of television instruction during the winter 1977 crisis was limited.

27. Mr. Frank Sabato.

**Local School
Arrangements**

It is a common research fallacy to assume that individual members have the same characteristics as the collective[1] and that once you understand something about the total system you automatically understand about the component parts. In the last chapter, specific variations in central office arrangements were identified which showed a difference in school system response to crisis. This chapter explores a second description of governmental arrangement which can be interpreted as the school system—the intraorganizational arrangement of local school centers.

Local school centers[2] in both the Columbus and Cincinnati school systems were identified by variables selected to give indication of (a) use of energy resources, (b) condition of existing facilities, and (c) use patterns of facilities. It was assumed that the following variables could show general differences and similarities of the intraorganizational arrangements which existed in "normal," non-crisis times.

a. Use of Energy Resources

    Type of heating fuel used (gas, coal, electric, oil, propane, and various combinations).

    Amount heating fuel used; all local school use was converted to British Thermal Units (BTUs) for standard description and comparisons. Each local school in both systems was described according to total yearly consumption (1976-77), monthly use for October 1976, February 1977, and April 1977.

    Amount of electricity used; all local school use was converted to kilowatts (KHW) and BTUs for standard comparisons. Each local school was described for 1976-77 yearly consumption.

    Square feet

b. Condition of Facilities

    Building age (to 1977).

    Location of site.

    Number of major alterations or renovations since construction.

    Enrollment capacity.

c.   Use of Facilities

Pupil utilization as percent of first-day 1977-78 enrollment to capacity.

Pupil to teacher ratio as average of number of regular teachers to pupil enrollment 1976-77.

Pupil mobility as percent of change in enrollment for 1976-77.

Comparisons within and between the local school centers of the two educational systems reveal some interesting differences. The average Cincinnati school was forty-two years old (to 1977), contained 79,100 square feet, had a fuel use (1976-77) of 5,646,000 BTUs, had an enrollment capacity of 897, and an actual building utilization of 63 percent. The average Columbus school was thirty-two years old (to 1977), contained 56,800 square feet, had a fuel use (1976-77) of 5,839,000 BTUs, had an enrollment capacity of 706, and an actual building utilization of 73 percent.

The figures suggest further internal variation in the type of impact an energy crisis would have on two school systems (both systems over 70 percent dependent on natural gas fuel for heating). On average, Columbus schools were newer, smaller, and utilized more efficiently than their Cincinnati counterparts. However, actual fuel use averaged the same (approximately) in both systems. This suggests that there was considerable variation among the local centers in each school system. The Cincinnati school centers ranged from buildings over 100 years old to six years old (to 1977). The smallest local school facility[3] had 5,300 square feet, a fuel use of 1,274,000 BTUs and an enrollment capacity of 180 pupils. The largest Cincinnati school center had 351,200 square feet, a fuel use of 30,969,000 BTUs, and an enrollment capacity of 3,050 pupils.

The Columbus local schools ranged from buildings over 100 years old to one put in use the year of the study (1977). The smallest local school had 21,300 square feet, a fuel use of 632,000 BTUs,[4] and an enrollment capacity of 270 pupils. The largest local school had 197,700 square feet, a fuel use of 30,169,000 BTUs and an enrollment capacity of 1,600 pupils.

These data suggest both school systems had distinct, internal differences among local school centers before the energy crisis of 1977. The warning for the research project was the need to document normal intraorganizational variation before assessing crisis response patterns. For example, it is interesting to note that Cincinnati schools had a facility with a pupil enrollment capactiy over 3,000, compared to a maximum Columbus building capacity of 1,600, yet the actual fuel use attributed to the largest facility in both systems was approximately the same for 1976-77.[5] Obviously, the operational meanings of "energy management" and "crisis response to winter conditions" would be very different in the administration of these two local school centers.

The internal differences between local school centers in both systems were also reflected in who used the facilities. The average Cincinnati local school had a pupil/teacher ratio of 23.3:1 and a pupil mobility rate of 35 percent. The average school contained 47 percent white pupils and 68 percent white teachers. The average Columbus local school had a pupil/teacher ratio of 29.4:1 and a pupil mobility rate of 14 percent. The average school had 66 percent white pupils and 82 percent white teachers at the time of this study.

Among the local schools in Cincinnati the pupil/teacher ratio ranged from 15.6:1 to 34.6:1; the pupil mobility rate ranged from zero to an astonishing 87 percent each year. Finally, the local schools ranged from those that had no white pupils to those that were 100 percent white and schools with a minimum of 55 percent white teachers to a maximum of 81 percent.

The pupil/teacher ratio in Columbus ranged from 17.1:1 to 38.8:1; the pupil mobility rate ranged from 2 percent to 63 percent. Some local schools had no white pupils while others were 100 percent white, and the percent of white teachers ranged from 71 percent to 94 percent.[6]

The study of normal intraorganizational variation due to differences in energy related variables within and between the local schools of Columbus and Cincinnati suggest different meanings of school system governance. This difference had to be clarified before analysis of crisis response could be understood. A representative sample of twelve Cincinnati schools and eleven Columbus schools was selected for intensive case study analyses.[7] (See appendix B for methodological format.) It was information derived from the twenty-one separate case studies that formed the basis of interpretation about local school governance arrangements during winter 1977.

Table 6-1 presents information regarding the representative nature of the eleven local schools of the Columbus sample.

As an example of how one would read the information in table 6-1, the

Table 6-1
The Columbus Local School Sample

Sample	School Organization[a]	Use of Energy Resources[b]	Condition of Facilities[c]	Use of Facilities[d]
Brookhaven	Senior high	5 of 156	126 of 156	15 of 156
Independence	Senior high	15 of 156	156 of 156	2 of 156
Mifflin	Senior high	17 of 156	51 of 156	4 of 156
Dominion	Junior high	27 of 156	94 of 156	93 of 156
Linmoor	Junior high	16 of 156	128 of 156	137 of 156
Alpine	Elementary	65 of 156	123 of 156	70 of 156
Chicago	Elementary	92 of 156	27 of 156	76 of 156
Gettysburg	Elementary	131 of 156	129 of 156	136 of 156
Northridge	Elementary	121 of 156	46 of 156	96 of 156
Ohio	Elementary	68 of 156	10 of 156	41 of 156
Parsons	Elementary	100 of 156	73 of 156	86 of 156

[a]Columbus has sixteen high schools (10-12), twenty-six junior high schools (7-9), and one hundred fourteen elementary schools.
[b]First indicates highest fuel use, largest square feet, highest electricity use.
[c]First indicates oldest building, largest number of modifications.
[d]First indicates largest percentage of first-day students to enrollment capacity.

Columbus sample contained three high schools, two junior highs, and six elementary schools. Independence, Brookhaven, and Mifflin high schools are large energy users, along with Linmoor junior high school. In contrast, Northridge elementary and Gettysburg elementary are small energy users. In "condition of facilities," Ohio elementary and Chicago elementary are among the oldest facilities, while Independence senior high was the newest facility in the Columbus system (at the time of this study). Finally, in actual utilization of facilities Independence and Mifflin senior highs have high pupil concentrations, while Linmoor junior high and Gettysburg elementary are among the most underutilized buildings in the Columbus system.

The Cincinnati sample consisted of twelve local schools, selected as representative on essentially the same critieria as the Columbus schools. Table 6-2 illustrates the relationship of the sample to the ninety-three local schools in the Cincinnati population of regular local schools.

Again, the reader can see that the Cincinnati sample contains two senior highs, one junior high, and nine elementary schools. Aiken and Western Hills senior highs, Gamble junior high, and Rockdale elementary are large fuel users. Burdett, Cummins, and Hoffman elementary schools are among the oldest schools in the Cincinnati system, while Rockdale elementary and Aiken senior high are among the newest facilities. Finally, Aiken and Western Hills high schools, Gamble junior high, and Westwood elementary are among the most utilized Cincinnati schools. In contrast, Garfield and Hoffman elementary schools are among the most underutilized schools.

In summary, a profile of all regular local schools in each school system was

Table 6-2
The Cincinnati Local School Sample

Sample	School Organization[a]	Use of Energy Resources[b]	Condition of Facilities[c]	Use of Facilities[d]
Aiken	Senior high	4 of 93	92 of 93	4 of 93
Western Hills	Senior high	2 of 93	10 of 93	2 of 93
Gamble	Junior high	17 of 93	61 of 93	10 of 93
Burdett	Elementary	73 of 93	1 of 93	38 of 93
Cummins	Elementary	74 of 93	3 of 93	49 of 93
Garfield	Elementary	44 of 93	27 of 93	81 of 93
Hoffman	Elementary	63 of 93	6 of 93	78 of 93
Kirby Road	Elementary	46 of 93	20 of 93	42 of 93
Mt. Washington	Elementary	61 of 93	49 of 93	56 of 93
Rockdale	Elementary	24 of 93	76 of 93	64 of 93
Avondale	Elementary	70 of 93	54 of 93	66 of 93
Westwood	Elementary	60 of 93	34 of 93	13 of 93

[a]Cincinnati has six high schools (two are 9-12), fourteen junior high schools, and seventy-one elementary schools.

[b]First indicates highest fuel use, largest square feet.

[c]First indicates oldest building, largest dependence on natural gas and/or coal fuel.

[d]First indicates largest percentage of first-day students to enrollment capacity and largest percentage of white pupils.

created, based upon their formal organization for curriculum, use of energy, condition of facilities, and use of facilities. The population profile demonstrated the need for the selection of a sample of local schools in each system to be studied for their particular intraorganizational governance arrangement and response to crisis during winter 1977. Eleven Columbus schools and twelve Cincinnati schools were selected for inividual case analyses of existing local school arrangements.

The Normal Local School Arrangement

Without the dimensions of crisis both local school samples exhibit considerable variation when described by select variables. Table 6-3 illustrates the normal variation of the Columbus sample.

All but one school is somewhat dependent upon natural gas for heating, so the pervasive impact of a winter 1977 type of crisis (for example, extreme need for heat and simultaneous shortage in fuel) can be easily seen. There are, however, other normal variations which could affect planning for other types of crisis. For example, building utilization percentages suggest a student "bulge" at the senior and junior high levels of schooling. Percent of pupil mobility (with the exception of Independence, which is a new school) seems generally related to percent of white pupils and percent of ADC pupils. Specifically, low mobility (that is, a "stable" school) was positively related to high white percentage and low ADC percentage. A planning model using these general variations would note Alpine elementary as a "deviation" (low ADC, low white, low pupil mobility).

In summary, the normal variations in the Columbus sample contain an implicit logic which could guide judgment in different types of crises. In fact, if the type of fuel could be ignored the "rational" decision posture for energy planning seems a function of calculating fuel use to square feet and enrollment capacity. The normal energy crisis decision process would lead to judgments of pupil rearrangements, specific conservation efforts in certain facilities, and so forth. However, the unavailability of natural gas in the dead of winter overrode all the normal variations and led to the logic of School Without Schools.

Table 6-4 outlines the normal variations in the Cincinnati sample. As Cincinnati attempted to replicate normal operations during winter 1977, intrinsic sample school variations are important to later infer "logical" judgments in "regular" crisis adaptation. Perhaps the most startling "built-in" variation is the relation between building utilization and percentage of white pupils. Six of the nine elementary schools in the sample had both less than 10 percent white pupils and a building utilization under 50 percent. Obviously, this normal variation could affect energy and any other type of crisis response to some extent. As we will see later (in the actual host-guest judgment involving South Avondale and Rockdale elementary schools), natural gas availability was not the sole criterion for crisis merging.

Table 6-3
Normal Variations within Columbus Sample

Sample	Type of Heating Fuel	Fuel Use (in BTUs rounded three places)	Electrical Use (in BTUs rounded three places)	Building Age (to 1977)	Square Feet (rounded two places)	Enrollment Capacity	Building Utilization (percent first day, 1977-78)	P/T Ratio	Percentage of White Teachers	Percentage of Pupils ADC	Percentage of Pupil Mobility	Percentage of White Pupils
Brookhaven Senior High	gas	12,841	3,091	14	1,573	1,350	100	27.8	91	4	3	88
Independence Senior High	electric	10,552[a]	9,999[b]	2	1,125	1,300	109	25.7	76	11	43	88
Mifflin Junior/Senior High	gas oil	9,493	3,116	53	1,178	1,200	124	26.5	79	38	25	38
Dominion Junior High	gas	7,089	1,236	21	836	850	81	26.9	90	2	6	89
Linmoor Junior High	gas	11,686	1,982	20	996	1,000	54	21.7	76	57	18	04
Alpine Elementary	gas	3,558	987	11	353	630	90	29.2	88	1	4	21
Chicago Elementary	gas	5,260	473	80	400	510	72	31.8	74	43	27	15
Gettysburg Elementary	gas	2,862	418	7	248	330	76	29.6	92	0	2	99
Northridge Elementary	gas oil	4,183	474	21	354	570	68	31.8	88	7	12	98
Ohio Elementary	gas	4,298	904	84	617	780	53	32.9	77	62	25	12
Parsons Elementary	gas	3,502	470	17	298	420	69	30.1	89	15	9	91

[a] As reported by central office; see note 4, this chapter.
[b] Maximum computer program parameter.

Table 6-4
Normal Variations within Cincinnati Sample

Sample	Type of Heating Fuel	Fuel Use (in BTUs rounded three places)	Electrical Use (in BTUs rounded three places)	Building Age (to 1977)	Square Feet (rounded two places)	Enrollment Capacity	Building Utilization (percent first day, 1977-78)	P/T Ratio	Percentage of White Teachers	Percentage of Pupils ADC	Percentage of Pupil Mobility	Percentage of White Pupils
Aiken Senior High	gas	14,489	5,047	15	1,182	1,960	91	15.7	80	15	24	47
Western Hills Senior High	gas oil coal	22,996	3,474	49	1,983	2,770	112	22.4	80	4	20	92
Gamble Junior High	coal	4,747	1,402	21	1,011	700	112	22.9	77	4	26	92
Burdett Elementary	gas coal	5,345	282	82	705	540	27	15.9	71	44	57	01
Cummins Elementary	gas coal	4,866	330	99	460	570	48	21.7	65	64	50	02
Garfield Elementary	coal	4,470	648	80	769	660	35	16.8	63	49	28	07
Hoffman Elementary	gas oil	2,900	812	55	639	600	44	21.4	56	64	35	00
Kirby Road Elementary	gas oil	2,828	581	67	647	630	86	26.0	68	32	33	75
Mt.Washington Elementary	gas	3,594	320	44	1,012	750	57	31.1	72	3	23	99
Rockdale Elementary	gas	5,174	1,160	22	678	1,100	36	15.8	65	47	41	01
Avondale Elementary	gas	2,894	403	27	398	630	49	19.5	62	60	36	00
Westwood Elementary	coal	3,997	424	68	652	600	101	28.6	69	5	19	99

In summary, both school system samples exhibit patterns of normal variations which could lead to inferences about "logical" crisis response. The normal
variation of Cincinnati and Columbus tends to suggest that some energy decisions may not be pure considerations but rather reflect previous student-related
data. On the other hand, the winter of 1977 unavailability of a particular type of
fuel which most of the Columbus local schools were dependent upon for heating
outstripped all normal variations and added a new, unique meaning to crisis decision-making. With these conclusions we now turn to variations in local school
arrangements directly attributed to winter 1977.

The Crisis Arrangements in Cincinnati

As noted earlier, the most significant adaptation efforts in Cincinnati related to
pupil transportation and local schools involved in the host-guest arrangements.
Four of the sample schools were not involved in either issue (all were "neighborhood" elementary schools, so most students did not ride school transportation
and none was affected as either host or guest) and were only affected by winter
1977 to the degree that heating fuel was natural gas. For example, Westwood
Elementary, which was totally dependent upon coal for heating, had no crisis in
1977. Respondents cited a new heating vent system as the most visible product
of the 1977 winter. The most unmanageable energy issue was perceived as uneven
heating (for example, some classrooms too hot), which is not too surprising for a
building almost seventy years old.

Hoffman, Kirby Road, and Burdett elementary schools were only partially
dependent on natural gas and not involved in host-guest arrangements. Respondents in these schools did not perceive the 1977 winter as an exceptional crisis.
Nonclassroom space which had to be heated (for example, auditoriums, hall-
ways), lack of insulation, and uneven heat were characteristic of energy concerns. There were no responses which dealt with particular school system issues
that occurred during January or February 1977.

From this sample, it could be inferred that some local schools which were
not significantly affected by transportation, host-guest arrangements, and other
(than natural gas) heating resources had no crisis in winter 1977. Administrators,
teachers, and classified personnel all reported that the Burdett, Kirby Road,
Hoffman, and Westwood elementary schools operated normally.

The Cincinnati sample included six schools which acted as hosts or received
students from other schools. Western Hills senior high had oil and coal heating to
augment natural gas while Gamble junior high, Garfield elementary, and Cummins elementary (partially) relied on coal resources. Two elementary sample
schools which received students (Mt. Washington and Rockdale) were totally
dependent on natural gas.[8]

Receiver schools in the Cincinnati sample did see the 1977 winter as a unique, crisis situation. Most of the energy problems cited were technical rather than human. Heating of nonclassroom space, lack of insulation, high ceilings, and uneven heating were characteristic concerns. Considering the number of pupils and staff involved in receiving people during the crisis there were few human-oriented concerns. There were several complaints about transportation (for example, students not picked up or lack of off-street parking) and the use of classrooms by guest teachers, but these were rare. The large majority of educators in the six host schools sampled were enthusiastic over the 1977 crisis response effort. Most felt the 1977 experience and local school crisis plans developed to take the "bugs out" of 1977 arrangements improved the crisis response capacity for future winters.

Finally, two sample schools sent their students and staff to other facilities as guests. Aiken senior high students were sent to a vocational school (in the same geographic location), while Avondale elementary students were guests in another elementary school (also a sample school, Rockdale). Although the information gathered from respondents was mixed, there were more negative comments from guests than other sample schools. In the guest school situations, several staff charged that the school system broke down and that skepticism was the most unmanageable problem for future crisis responses.

Several conclusions about winter 1977 can be made concerning the results of this study of Cincinnati sample schools. First, there was no pervasive crisis over energy which would provide a basis to talk legitimately of how the Cincinnati school system responded as a unitary organization. Certain local schools were unaffected by the 1977 winter. Other local schools (those who acted as hosts) minimized the detrimental aspects of the winter crisis and were pleased with their adaptation efforts. Finally, there is some indication that guest schools may have felt the adverse effects of winter 1977 more that other local schools in the system.

However, a second conclusion, based upon sample results, would be that local school respondents were pleased with the crisis response effort in winter 1977. Complaints were scattered, but few had to do with issues which could be labeled "administration" or "planning." In fact, the role of the Cincinnati central office was perceived in a most positive fashion. Terms such as "sympathetic," "concerned," and "helpful" were used to describe the central office role. This is an important finding, for the actual governance role of the Cincinnati central office *vis-à-vis* the local schools would be characterized as indirect and often *laissez-faire* (see chapter 8 for specific decision examples). Especially during February 1977, local school centers operated with a high degree of decision autonomy. Apparently, local school personnel felt that the lack of central office control was appropriate in adapting to the winter 1977 crisis.

In conclusion, the perspective of local governance arrangements which is based upon the results of a study of a select sample of schools is different from a central office perspective of the same arrangement. Intraorganizational variation in crisis response at the local school seems both a function of "natural" differences and specific adaptation arrangements for a particular site. In 1977, local school incumbents who were guests in the Cincinnati adaptation effort seemed to bear more detrimental effects than their colleagues in host roles or those not involved in host-guest arrangements.

We now turn to the crisis response efforts undertaken by a sample of Columbus local schools during winter 1977.

The Crisis Arrangement in Columbus

As explained earlier, the Columbus system implemented School Without Schools, which affected all local schools to some extent during February. Part of the School Without Schools reorganization (which affected all local schools) was the introduction of a third tier of administration. The third tier was composed of "clusters" of local school centers which operated between individual sites and the central office during the crisis adaptation. A basic purpose of School Without Schools was to reduce the occupancy and use of natural gas heated schools, yet continue to provide educational opportunities for Columbus children. Certain local schools with other than gas heating arrangements were selected to operate full time so that pupils and staff from closed (gas heated) schools could meet for classes one day per week at those locations. The school operating full time was the cluster center for the number of closed schools using the facility.[9] The clusters varied from three to six schools and functioned to provide mail service and a location for food services and administrative coordination among local schools. One of the Columbus sample schools, Independence Senior High, was a cluster center because it was electrically heated. Members of the other sample schools met in alternative facilities for one day per week classes.

One of the highlights of the School Without Schools adaptation effort was the administrative functioning of the cluster tier of government. Cluster coordination was the responsibility of the local school administrators assigned to a particular grouping. During the month of crisis, cluster teams of elementary, junior high, and senior high administrators made joint decisions regarding the use of the center location. All sample respondents (particularly the principals of sample schools) perceived the emergency operation of the clusters as one of the major successes of School Without Schools. Several respondents commented that the decentralized emergency cluster operation allowed local school administrators to communicate much more effectively and decide more efficiently than the normal government arrangement of central office to individual local schools. This implies that curricular and instructional decisions (for example, class scheduling) were perceived as appropriate cluster level concerns while other decisions (for example, athletic events, food service, television, buses for field trips) were the purview of specialized central office operations.

We will see in following chapters that each local school in Columbus had its own particular set of School Without Schools experiences. Curriculum, instruction, and use of personnel varied as each teacher and local school adminstrator interpreted the constraints and opportunities of one day per week classes, use of television and radio, use of field trips, and so forth. Patterns of intraorganizational variation can only be inferred after the fact because there was no planned, system-wide variation among local schools during the month of crisis. The true units of analysis to describe most of the crisis adaptation which took place were the classroom and individual teacher. However, ex post facto study of student attendance percentages during School Without Schools reveals three general variations among the eleven sample schools. The normal attendance percentage of all Columbus pupils is somewhere between 92 and 95 percent on a given day. During School Without Schools, the overall attendance percentage varied between 76 and 85 percent. On the first day of the first week of School Without Schools implementation four sample schools reported attendance over 90 percent (Independence Senior, Dominion Junior, Alpine Elementary, and Gettysburg Elementary), one reported attendance below 70 percent (Ohio Elementary), and the others were in between (Brookhaven, Mifflin, Linmoor, Chicago, Northridge, and Parsons). On the first day of the third week of School Without Schools only three sample schools reported better than 90 percent attendance (Dominion, Alpine, and Gettysburg). Those sample schools reporting less than 70 percent attendance had risen to five (Brookhaven Senior, Mifflin Senior, Linmoor Junior, Chicago Elementary, and Ohio Elementary). These data seem to indicate that the effort spent in actual implementation of School Without Schools served to differentiate local schools on the basis of pupil attendance in one class per week activities. On this criterion it seems that certain local schools were becoming less enthusiastic than others by the third week of emergency operation.

One positive characteristic that respondents of all sample schools reported to be an outcome of the one day per week classes was the ability to maintain some continuity of learning by direct contact with students. One common complaint of all sample school respondents was the lack of time available to teach under the one day per week arrangement.[10]

There was some differentiation among sample schools based upon the *type* of specific problem identified with one day per week classes. The secondary and junior high schools reported problems of student discipline, laboratory arrangements, and athletic scheduling. Sample elementary schools that had less than 70 percent attendance by the third week (Ohio, Chicago, Linmoor) mentioned specific problems with students (especially attendance, lunchroom discipline, and overcrowded classes), while sample elementary schools which were above 90 percent attendance in the third week did not mention students as a particular problem.

Finally, only the elementary sample school respondents reported specific problems of lack of supplies and availability of materials to conduct classes one day per week.

The following responses to the School Without Schools local school arrangement infer the general conclusion that understanding of the winter 1977 impact is most appropriate on a case-by-case basis. Brookhaven senior and Mifflin senior respondents would require mandatory pupil attendance, require homework, and have classes at least two or three times a week. Linmoor, Ohio, and Gettysburg elementary school respondents wanted specific system-wide guidelines for emergency operations (beyond the *Handbook*). On the other hand, Alpine elementary respondents were appreciative of the lack of system-wide guidelines.

Independence Senior High respondents (the only sample school serving a cluster facility) noted that there was no "fair warning" and a lack of preplanning. Gettysburg and Alpine elementary schools apparently had problems with television units while at Chicago and Parsons elementary schools the issues were bus schedules and gas allotments for field trips.

The last bit of information relevant to the sample perspective of local school arrangements in Columbus concerns the perceived success of the effort. Only respondents at Brookhaven senior high and Alpine elmentary were unanimous in the opinion that School Without Schools had improved their crisis response capacity. Over half of the respondents at Dominion junior high (one of the schools with 90 percent attendance in the third week), Northridge elementary, and Parsons elementary were unsure or did not feel their crisis response ability was improved by the 1977 winter effort. More to the point, *skepticism* was mentioned as the most unmanageable area of future crisis adaptation by at least two respondents from Brookhaven, Independence, and Mifflin senior highs, Dominion junior high and Linmoor, Chicago, and Parsons elementary schools.

In conclusion, the lack of consistent, pervasive patterns of response among sample schools could support the inference of extreme decentralized local school arrangements throughout School Without Schools. Although speculations have been attempted, concrete description suggests that the story of School Without Schools adaptation is somewhat unique to each local school setting. Further, it was impossible to differentiate many issues and concerns identified with School Without Schools from the normal problems faced by a particular site. For example, sample schools citing student attendance as a crisis response issue were approximately the same schools that were most affected by this problem (*vis-à-vis* the rest of the sample) in noncrisis times.

Summary

This chapter presented a perspective of local school governance arrangements which may help to make inferences about intraorganizational variations in both systems. Variables selected to describe the use of energy resources, condition of facilities, and use of facilities suggest that considerable "normal" variation exists between and within the local school centers of the two school systems. A sample of representative schools selected from each system further illustrated existing variations among local schools. The 1977 winter was a crisis of shortage in a type of fuel. Where all Columbus local schools were affected by this fact, a good percentage of Cincinnati local schools were not. Even for those Cincinnati schools requiring some emergency adaptation (the role of receiver or host school) the 1977 winter was not perceived as especially disruptive. Only members of sample schools which were required to be guests of other facilities during the 1977 winter were skeptical about the emergency arrangements.

In Columbus, all local school arrangements were affected by School Without Schools. The creation of clusters of local schools as an intermediate government was well received as an emergency arrangement. Although sample schools shared some similarities and overall differences it was most difficult to generalize about adaptation efforts. This implies that Columbus local schools operated in virtual decision autonomy during February 1977. Finally, regardless of the particular adaptation made, there was considerable skepticism among sample school respondents as to the value of future School Without Schools efforts.

In the last two chapters, we have attempted to describe the crisis response of 1977 from the organizational perspective of central office and local school center. The following chapters continue the analysis of crisis response from a decision-making perspective. We start with decisions concerning fuel and transportation.

Notes

1. Related to this fallacy are the issues of data aggregation and identifying the unit of analysis.

2. It was beyond the capacity of this research effort to include special schools, vocational schools, and other facilities not identified with the "regular" elementary, junior high, or senior high school instructional program.

3. "Smallest" and "largest" are composites of the extreme characteristics that existed at the time of this study rather than the actual description of a single facility.

4. There was considerable disgreement among Columbus officials as to how fuel consumption was attributed to particular local facilities. The fuel use statistic presented also reflects the results of School Without Schools, which altered the normal use of certain facilities for a month.

5. Again, the real issue may be one of "creative accounting" in presentation of this statistic.

6. At the time of this study both school systems were under legal challenge for failure to desegregate.

7. A factor analysis of all local school variables under study identified several clusters which guided sample selection. Besides the type of school organiza-

tion, local schools were selected for a gross representation of various energy use (a combination of fuel use, square feet to be heated, and electrical use), condition of facilities (age and number of structural modifications to buildings), and use of facilities (percent of first-day students of 1977 school year to enrollment capacity).

8. There seems little consistent reasoning as to the selection of these schools as hosts (rather than guests) except that they were both small users and probably could have been designated either way.

9. There were exceptions to this general finding. For example, seven Columbus schools met one day per week in a nonschool facility. Two of the sample schools, Parsons and Alpine elementary, met in nonschool facilties.

10. Alpine elementary, which met in a nonschool facility, substituted meeting one and one-half hours each for five days each week rather than one normal school day (five hours) per week.

7

System-wide Planning and Decision-making

To this point, intraorganizational and interorganizational variations have been described in relation to select environmental and school system variables. Another perspective about the way Cincinnati and Columbus schools responded to winter 1977 identifies specific plans and decision processes utilized in adaptation efforts. This chapter describes the crisis response of the two school systems to four decision issues: (1) alleviating natural gas heating needs, (2) securing pupil transportation, (3) modifiying personnel agreements, and (4) receiving compensation from the State Department of Education. The resolution of each issue identifies specific variations in how the two school systems implemented plans and procedures for emergency adaptation.

Natural Gas Heating Needs

In chapter 3, the critical relation of natural gas unavailability to the severity of crisis for existing school arrangements was established. Natural gas was the schools systems' "lifeblood" for heating because each school jurisdiction was over 70 percent dependent upon this particular fuel. Previous discussion also showed that the shortage of natural gas was much more pronounced for Columbus schools than in Cincinnati. This fact contributed to the policy decision to implement a total, system-wide adaptation effort in the Columbus case and a decision to limit the impact of winter 1977 to one-fourth of the school system in the Cincinnati situation. With this review and the consideration of specific decision events (see appendix A) it is possible to discuss plans and procedures which were affected by fuel needs.

Conservation

Before the 1977 winter both the Columbus and the Cincinnati schools had plans for the general conservation of natural gas. The plans had been created in response to internal audits of actual natural gas consumption and a review of current heating, ventilation, and lighting practices in the local schools of each system. The procedures to guide conservation efforts in both school systems identified the following major types of local school activities: lower water temperatures in boilers (for classroom heating and cafeteria needs), reduce fresh air ventilation,[1] lower thermostats to "sweater comfort" heating, limit entrances and exits during arrival and departure times, turn off incandescent and fluorescent lights, reduce corridor lighting, and decorate all rooms with light colors that reflect light.

The actual implementation of conservation efforts in both school systems prior to winter 1977 was guided by two assumptions. First, most conservation activities were technical and the primary responsibility of local school custodians or central office plant maintenance/operations personnel. Second, the extent of conservation effort needed was to be governed by the anticipated curtailment of base allocations by the schools' public utility. In Columbus, "large user" local school allocations were curtailed 40 percent for the 1975 and 1976 winters and the school system conserved enough to absorb those curtailments within the parameters of needed fuel supplies prior to 1977. It was not until the curtailment was raised to 50 percent in January 1977 that the existing conservation plan of the Columbus schools was proved inadequate.

In Cincinnati, the public utility notified the schools that they could expect up to a 28 percent curtailment of large user base allocations, but no actual curtailmant of natural gas was implemented until winter 1977 (and then the initial curtailment was 20 percent). In response to the call for voluntary conservation, the Cincinnati schools had, like Columbus, made significant decreases in the actual natural gas needed to heat facilities.

From a planning perspective, the long-range conservation effort in both systems cannot be faulted for failure to make what seemed to be necessary adjustments to original heating practices. The conservation efforts did not call for large-scale involvement of teachers, adminstrators, and students because the technical adjustments seemed adequate to meet anticipated fuel shortages. Prior to winter 1977, efforts to mobilize the bulk of professional educators and students in conservation activities was not an integral part of adaptive planning. When the implication of extreme fuel shrotage became apparent in mid-January 1977, there were some hasty efforts to induce massive conservation by all participants in the school system. Local school thermostats were lowered, plans for emergency use of buildings were distributed, and the superintendents of both school systems made direct appeals for personal sacrifice.

The actual effect of the winter 1977 emergency conservation effort can only be inferred for both school systems. Columbus closed most natural gas heated local schools which, in effect, made the actual cooperation of educators and students less important than in Cincinnati, which attempted to operate normally. In unused Columbus facilities, conservation efforts were under the control of the custodians and the primary focus was to maintain the "mothballed" condition[2] of the plants. For the most part, Cincinnati schools maintained normal occupancy and the direct effects of natural gas shortage were limited to a subportion of the total system. This may be the reason why some efforts to involve individuals in personal conservation of heating were somewhat hampered in Cincinnati. Our study of Cincinnati local schools found several teachers and even local administrators who did not appreciate the *system-wide* problem of heating. Particularly in local schools not heated by natural gas, there were some complaints of *overheating* and the need to open windows to make certain classrooms livable.[3] One implication that this finding suggests is the potential difficulty of achieving mass conservation efforts by educators even during actual emergencies. The uneven heating within buildings and the differential impact of heating shortage (caused by absence of a particular fuel) among buildings did make some Cincinnati occupants skeptical of system-wide needs to conserve energy during winter 1977.

Converting to an Alternative Fuel

A second area where plans and procedures for securing heating needs were affected was the conversion of natural gas to alternative fuels. Conversion efforts were related to both the ongoing building program within the school system and to its energy supplier for natural gas.

A building characteristic of both school systems was that the older the local school facility, the more likely the heating was not natural gas. Natural gas and electricity were the two "modern" heating fuels while coal and oil heating were characteristic of "old-time" heating efforts. As noted in an earlier chapter, Columbus schools were newer, designed on a smaller scale of people per site, and better maintained than Cincinnati schools. Consequently, although both school systems were more than 70 percent dependent on natural gas overall, the actual impact of dependency on a school-to-school basis reflected a different pattern. Most of the newer Columbus schools were natural gas heated, while most of the Cincinnati schools (the system had not built a new school for ten years up to the time of this study) were heated by older fuels. More important to the planning of fuel conversion, several Cincinnati schools that were heated by natural gas in 1976 and 1977 still retained an older heating system which could be reactivated. In response to winter 1977 both systems attempted emergency conversion of the heating units in local schools. Cincinnati was able to convert four natural gas schools in a short period of time because another heating system was already installed. "Obsolete" coal bins were refilled, oil tanks were replenished, and boilers were converted back to original heating arrangements. Although this flexbility had not been anticipated or planned in a proactive manner, it did have a direct impact upon the capacity of the Cincinnati schools to achieve emergency conversion.

A second aspect of converting local facilities to other than natural gas heating was the effect on existing supply arrangements between the schools and the utilities. As discussed earlier, natural gas supply is determined by the type of user[4] a customer is and the base allocation established for that customer. In Ohio, school districts could pool or aggregate the amounts of natural gas to be received by individual facilities into general accounts.[5] For example, the amount of gas to be received by all large user schools was reported and supplied by the public utility as a single base allocation account rather than individual schools or specific gas meters on site.

The relationship between a school system's base allocation of natural gas and plans to convert particular facilities to alternative fuel is demonstrated by the Columbus "phantom school" practice. Even prior to the emergency conditions of winter 1977, Columbus schools received base allocations of gas for local facilities that had been closed or no longer housed children. This was possible by keeping a gas meter at the unused site. If the flow of gas was enough to keep a pilot light burning this was sufficient to keep a facility classified as "operating" for base allocation purposes by the utility. The actual use of fuel by a particular site was lost in the aggregate total of the pooled user account. School officials rationalized this practice with the argument that the original base allocation was established in an arbitrary manner and that a 1974 base had little relation to the actual gas needs in 1977.

The possible relation of this practice of "creative accounting" to plan for emergency fuel conversion is obvious. Total conversion from natural gas costs the school system the base allocation amount for that facility. However, retaining gas meters at the same site allows a school system to continue to receive a base allocation amount while actually heating the site by an alternative fuel arrangement.

Augmenting Natural Gas Supplies

A third area of planning to secure heating fuel needs concerned the augmenting of available natural gas supplies. Three specific considerations in this decision area were the "carryover" of fuel allocations and the securing of self-help gas. Carryover was an idea that originated before shortages became a way of life. A school system's allocation is divided into two seasons, heating season and non-heating season. Although gas allocations are calculated monthly, there is also a maximum allocation for each season. For example, the Columbus heating season runs from November 3 to April 3.

Natural gas is a type of fuel that requires that a minimum volume be maintained, both at points of general distribution and of specific delivery. Prior to winter 1977, public utilities would find that certain season allocations would not be used or some other unexpected factor would cause surplus gas to become available. This carryover gas could be purchased by customers at a negotiated price and used to supplement another season's allocation.

In October 1976, a curious event took place. Columbia Gas of Ohio offered the Columbus schools a supply of summer carryover natural gas. This offer took place at the same time the company was warning of the strict enforcement of mandatory curtailment of heating season (winter) allocations. Further, the summer carryover gas was offered at a considerably higher price than regular season allocations. The Columbus school officials, not expecting the drastic conditions which were to follow three months later, did not purchase the carryover supplies.

The planning implication of the carryover phenomenon is that season allocation and actual availability may not coincide. In fact, a school system may be able to secure carryover amounts from the same supplier (and at the same time) who has imposed strict curtailment levels or is reducing base allocation levels.

A second means to augment available supplies of natural gas was attempted by Columbus schools in winter 1977. Due to the 1977 crisis, P.U.C.O. (state utilities commission) ruled that self-help gas could be used to heat boilers as a special, one-time exception (to the normal use of only in forced air or space heating arrangements).[6] This modification convinced Columbus planners that efforts to secure self-help gas were worthwhile.

Schools can enter into a self-help augmentation under three conditions: through direct contact with the gas producer, if the system owns its own gas wells (for example, Cleveland tried to drill its own), or if two or more districts (or a district and another industry) want to enter into a joint venture. There are several basic problems to all three arrangements. First, even though self-help gas often comes from intrastate wells, there is no limit in the cost of such gas which a producer (driller) might charge. During 1977, P.U.C.O. only monitored gas transmission (intra- and interstate), so it confined its judgments to contracts between a school district and a public utility. In short, producers who drill for the self-help gas could charge what the traffic would bear.

Second, the amount of self-help gas during the winter 1977 crisis was significant in relation to need. The efforts to create such arrangements had the utilities (as transmitters) putting in additional pipes and meters, while various legal restrictions at the state and federal levels created too much of a time lag. During 1977, Columbus schools went to extreme ends to secure self-help supplies but the total gas resources actually found was less than 5 percent of annual usage.

Third, the school system was most dependent on external agencies and expertise in its efforts to secure self-help supplies. Columbus used a nonprofit corporation, Gas, Inc., to explore the self-help option for itself and several school districts in the metropolitan area. The corporation negotiated with various producers of existing wells and drillers of anticipated wells (in Ohio and other states), bargained with Columbia Gas of Ohio to transmit found gas and handled all major decision functions.

Summary

Both Columbus and Cincinnati schools engaged in planning and decision activities designed to deal with the issue of meeting natural gas heating needs. Efforts were concentrated in the broad policy areas of fuel conservation, the conversion of natural gas heating to alternative fuels, and the augmentation of available natural gas supplies. The specific plans and practices of the two school systems in these areas revealed some commonalities. Both Columbus and Cincinnati initially considered fuel conservation a technical concern and planned adaptive efforts in light of anticipated curtailments in base allocations of natural gas. Second, both systems attempted to convert particular facilities to alternative fuels when the severe nature of winter 1977 became apparent.

However, the two school systems also exhibited considerable differences in what and how decisions were made about natural gas needs. The effort by Cincinnati to replicate normal school operations meant certain local school facilities were occupied during the crisis months which might have been mothballed under a different plan. Efforts by central office and local school administrators to secure voluntary compliance to harsh conservation measures (for example, classroom temperature at 60°) had mixed results and only partial success.

A second difference was the energy benefit Cincinnati schools gained for not having an updated and systematic facility building program. Most of the Cincinnati schools that had natural gas heating also had an alternative fuel system installed but not at work (this system also had a larger number of schools that did not have the modern fuels of natural gas or electricity). Conversion to alternative fuel meant reactivating the obsolete heating system rather than installing a new heating system in a particular facility.

Another difference was the practice of Columbus schools of maintaining certain local facilities (which had been calculated in the original natural gas base allocation) to secure allocations of gas even when the building no longer served an educational function. This allowed the school system to use the amounts allocated to phantom schools (where only a meter and pilot light existed) in the aggregate pool of gas resources.

A final difference between the school systems was the extent to which Columbus pursued the self-help gas option in hopes of augmenting curtailed amounts of this fuel. This decision was consistent with other efforts by the Columbus schools to obtain resources from its external environment.

Pupil Transportation Needs

Another issue where decision processes and concerns were different with respect to crisis adaptation was pupil transportation. In Cincinnati the issue involved three phases; the "make do" efforts of early January 1977 before the schools recognized the crisis, the provision of transportation during the host-guest experiment, and the attempt to rationalize emergency transportation for state compensation after the winter.

Between January 3, 1977, when schools began the second semester and the beginning of the host-guest arrangement on February 8, 1977, the Cincinnati pupil transportation decision process was, in effect, a single-person operation. The transportation coordinator handled the critical negotiations for service with the city municipal transit, private contracted buses, and cab companies. The major problems during this time (January) were questions about insurance coverage to transport children under hazardous conditions and the day-to-day decision as to whether the Cincinnati schools would be operating. As the crisis days of January evolved, the transportation coordinator became the actor who checked the weather conditions, checked the abilities of various transportation systems to operate, and then recommended to the superintendent whether schools should operate.

The host-guest arrangement broadened the participation of Cincinnati administrators in pupil transportation decisions. Although the host-guest plan was to minimize the effects of crisis, the pairing arrangement still involved twenty-five local schools and 20,000 pupils to be transported. Schedules for emergency transportation were negotiated (primarily by the transportation coordinator) to a final decision which involved issuing extra tokens for pupils riding municipal buses, twenty extra contracted buses to operate on triple shifts, and twenty extra taxi trips provided each school day.

The third phase occurred when Cincinnati attempted to pursuade the State Department of Education that additional reimbursement for emergency transportation during the crisis was a legitimate compensation. Although the emergency transportation cost Cincinnati schools approximately $1,800 a day in extra expense, SDE would not honor the costs.[7]

In contrast to the Cincinnati effort to provide pupil transportation, the Columbus venture was a cornerstone of the School Without Schools plan.[8] School Without Schools was to provide Columbus pupils one day of regular classes in their cluster school and four days of "alternative activities." Two main components of alternative activities were radio-television programming and field trips in the Columbus metropolitan area. The central office staff, under the coordination of the emergency operations center, would process all teacher requests for transportation in field trip activities. A team of seven administrators provided continuous coordination of pupil transportation throughout the three weeks of School Without Schools. At the end of the crisis adaptation, 99,697 pupils had been provided centrally scheduled field trips.

In retrospect, the contrast of pupil transportation decisions in Cincinnati and Columbus seems a vivid demonstration of how critical services were provided for in the two systems. As it turned out, the transportation of pupils was imperative for both the replication of normal governance in Cincinnati and to implement the Columbus School Without Schools. In this light, the Cincinnati arrangement was much more tentative, crisis prone, and unplanned than the Columbus provision of pupil transportation in winter 1977.

Modified Personnel Arrangements

A third area where the school systems exhibited different plans and procedures was the modification of existing personnel agreements to cope with crisis.

Cincinnati central office administrators made no effort to change existing contractual arrangements between teaching and classified personnel during winter 1977. Instead, the superintendent of schools relied on particular sections of the existing contracts to justify emergency modifications of normal arrangements. Sections 4116.24 and 4216.24 of the Board of Education and Cincinnati Federation of Teachers reads:

> When a school day is shortened or cancelled for students owing to emergency conditions, *all employees scheduled to work are expected to work as usual. The superintendent may authorize these exceptions:*
>
> Certificated school-based employees, such as teachers, counselors, and administrators, whom the superintendent judges can work productively at home, *may be advised* to do so instead of reporting to or remaining at their schools. Principals so advised will, however, remain responsible for the security of their schools and for seeing that their buildings and grounds are made as ready as possible for school on the next scheduled day.
>
> Non-certificated school-based employees, such as instructor assistants, clerical employees, and lunchroom employees, whose reporting to or remaining at work is in the superintendent's judgment not in the interest of the system, may be advised not to remain or report.
>
> Employees authorized under the above exceptions not to report for or remain at work will be paid as if they had worked as usual. (emphasis added)[9]

In the actual implementation of these sections during winter 1977, the superintendent declared that inclement weather closing of schools meant no teachers or lunchroom personnel would report for work but building plant operators, custodians, and janitorial employees would be required to be on duty. All central office employees worked during the closed days and principals "remain responsible for the security of their buildings and seeing that their schools are ready as possible for the next scheduled day."

In summarizing the actual operations of personnel during the crisis, a central office administrator stated:

> No employee was required to do anything outside his or her contract during the energy crisis. . . . The existing negotiated contract stipulates that the Federation shall be involved in any revisions of the wording of regular or supplemental contracts. . . . Several individuals voluntarily did more than that which was specified in the contract, although in most cases that was not necessary. The responsibility of teachers was compacted in time, but remained the same. Principals had longer hours in some cases but responsibilities were not changed. Since the length of

time for teachers was not exceeded, their contracts were not violated. Time is not a part of an administrator's contract. All civil service employees continued working. In some cases, particularly cooks, secretaries, and a few custodians, work has continued at a different place, but it remained of the same kind.[10]

In contrast to the Cincinnati version of emergency adaptation, Columbus schools engaged in formal contractual modifications for winter 1977. Article 1101 of the master contract between the Columbus board and teacher federation at the time of this study outlined the process for altering existing personnel arrangements.

> The President of the Association and the Superintendent may meet privately during the term of this Agreement for the purpose of discussing the amendment of this Agreement. In the event this discussion produces a mutual accord that a specific amendment is desirable, such proposal for amendment will be referred to the Joint Negotiating Committee and if the amendment is mutually agreed upon by the joint committee, it will be submitted for ratification by the Board of Education and a policy-making body of the Board of Education and a policy-making body of the Association. No public discussion or disclosure of the desire for amendment shall take place prior to or unless mutually agreed to be submitted to the Joint Committee.[11]

Obviously, the article was worded to make amendment a deliberate, systematic process which emphasized caution and restraint by both board and federation. As the conditions of January 1977 forced the realization of a true energy shortage and the need for immediate crisis adaptation, a different amendment process took place. Rather than a time-consuming process dominated by the formal and legal intricacies of committee consideration, amendments during winter 1977 involved only two persons and but four days. Trust and mutual respect gained from previous board and federation confrontation were attributed to the decision that federation members were to be involved in all aspects of School Without Schools planning (before and during the crisis) and that the critical master contract modifications would occur with unprecedented speed.

On January 30, 1977, an emergency memorandum of agreement outlined the following personnel guidelines;

1. The Columbus Board of Education and the teachers of the Columbus Public Schools, represented by the Columbus Education Association, shall endeavor, during the period of emergency closing to provide the best possible education for pupils of the school system under the emergency conditions by utilizing available community school system facilities and resources.

2. During the period of emergency closing teachers shall be assigned duties or shall undertake duties usually associated with the teach-

ing profession and shall not be assigned duties of a "make work" nature, extensive clerical duties, or assignments not usually associated with the teaching profession.

3. Participation in the programs designed for presentation in the media shall be on a voluntary basis.

4. Participation in activities beyond the normal work day of teachers shall be on a voluntary basis.

5. Teachers shall have no less than the normal preparation, planning, and lunch periods provided during the regular school year, on a weekly average.

6. A joint Conflict Resolution Committee, composed of four members shall be established to expedite the relolution of problems related to the emergency closing of programs and activities arising therefrom. The committee shall report at least weekly to the Superintendent and the President of the Columbus Education Association and shall operate under the rules for joint committees set forth in Article 508 of the CEA-Board Master Agreement.

The abstractness of the amendments was somewhat clarified by the "School Without Schools" *Handbook* which attempted to establish specific teacher role expectations.

1. Pupils and teachers are expected to have at least one day "in-school" together each week between February 7 and 25.

2. Teachers are expected to arrange for as many additional activities involving pupils as possible, including lessons in the media, visits to community facilities, and such activities as they are able to create.

3. Pupils are expected to participate in all scheduled School Without Schools activities, and parents are expected to help see that they do.

4. All school personnel are expected to use maximum creativity in making assignments and maintaining contacts with pupils.

5. Throughout the School Without Schools project, school personnel are expected to help pupils and parents be fully informed about:

    The Columbus Public Schools building their school is assigned to use one day per week.

    The bus schedule for the "in-school" day.

    Lesson assignments.

    Learning opportunities available through television, radio, the newspapers, and community facilities.

    How teachers and pupils can stay in touch with one another.

Note: The expectations listed above also apply to situations in which a school will have its "in-school" day in a community facility.

6. Pupils are expected to be present when their school is scheduled for its "in-school" day. Normal excuses for absence will be accepted.

7. Teachers are expected to determine whom to call in case of emergency while a pupil is in school or participating in a School Without Schools activity.

8. Pupils are expected to take textbooks home, as instructed by their teachers.

9. Pupils are expected to complete assignments made by their teachers during the School Without Schools project.

10. Teachers are expected to take attendance at all scheduled School Without Schools activities.

11. Teachers are expected to record grades on the performance of pupils on assignments made and tests given during the project.

12. Teachers are expected to keep themselves available for professional assignments as needed.[12]

It should be noted that, beyond taking attendance, recording grades, and keeping oneself available, there was no stipulation of actual teaching activities during the crisis period. This omission was by design, as emphasized by the weekly teacher newspaper:

Reporting Teaching Activities. The *only* reporting to be required of teachers regarding their activity during this unusual crisis is a report which will be given to all teachers upon their return to their schools following a return to normalcy. The form will simply ask teachers to identify the number of days they used sick leave, or other leave days, and to sign that they were available for assignment on all other days. If you are asked to make any other kind of accounting or report, you are to notify the Conflict Resolution Committee.[13]

The success of the emergency modification can be inferred from the teacher's perspective given after the School Without Schools effort.

It would be a miracle if such a drastic alteration in the operation of schools did not create some severe labor-management difficulties, and so the Joint CEA-Board Conflict Resolution Committee was built into the structure of the crisis program during its advance planning. But to date, the committee has not had to be used. There have been misunderstandings and problems to be solved to be sure; but it is to the credit of teachers and administrators, CEA and the Administration alike that there has been such a spirit of cooperation and determination to make the program succeed that conflicts have been resolved so far without having to resort to using the formal structure. That cooperation was fostered by the invitation to CEA President to participate in the daily meetings of the Superintendent's Cabinet (which involved CEA in the highest level of decisionmaking and created a context in which CEA could legitimately support the program while serving its members); the cooperation extended to communication and support between the publication staffs of the CEA and the Board, including their sharing of photographs with the *Voice*, and actually printing two issues of this newsletter in which CEA cooperated in the task of improving the lines of communication between the Superintendent and the teachers of the school system.[14]

This positive relationship between the teachers and central administration remained throughout the 1977 winter.

Modifications of the existing contract with classified personnel were somewhat less amicable. The general tenor of the central office was "If you want to get paid, don't argue about what you're doing." The following excerpt from the administrative agreement stipulates the choice for not working by public employees.

EMERGENCY GUIDELINES

The emergency closing of many school buildings may result in an interruption in the normal work activities of some educational aides and classified employees such as food service personnel. Such employees should first be offered work within their classification. If such work is not available employees should be offered other reasonably suitable work. The hours of work offered will be at least equal to the employee's regular scheduled hours if the work offered is on an overtime basis. *If employees who are so reassigned elect an unpaid status for the period of the emergency they shall do so without loss of paid holidays which occur during the emergency period.* (emphasis added)[15]

No classified employee elected a "nonpaid status" and no grievances were filed during the 1977 winter crisis.

In summary, decisions regarding the modification of personnel arrangements reflected the larger policy dynamics of the two school systems. Cincinnati attempted to minimize the unusual nature of winter 1977 and decided that existing contractual arrangements were satisfactory for crisis adjustments. Columbus schools felt the need to emphasize the unique nature of winter 1977 as a rationale to modify existing arrangements among school personnel. We now turn to a final area of system-wide decision-making which exhibits how Columbus and Cincinnati differed in the relationship to the State Department of Education.

Relations with the State Department of Education

Previous discussion has established that the Ohio State Department of Education (hereafter SDE) had considered energy shortage an educational issue three years prior to winter 1977 and had played an advocacy role in state politics for the securing of energy supplies for public schools. It was also noted that SDE took a special and direct relationship to the Columbus public schools that was not replicated with Cincinnati or other Ohio school districts.

After winter 1977, SDE played an important decision role in judging whether emergency actions taken by local districts could receive special compensation. If crisis actions could be rationalized as legitimate extra expense, the Ohio legislature and other state agencies had provided financial resources for qualifying districts.[16] SDE judged the nature of local district qualification based upon the criterion of whether emergency actions were equivalent to normal or conventional school operations. The school system that could justify emergency actions in conventional rationales stood to gain considerable compensation in dollars. In this case study, Columbus was found to be extremely successful in creating a rationale for reimbursement; Cincinnati was not. As discussed earlier, the Ohio legislature passed an emergency bill to reimburse local districts up to fifteen days for "lack of or potential lack of fuel." Later legislation also legitimized possible reimbursement for days missed for "hazardous weather." Both compensatory efforts were clear that no more than fifteen days could be claimed. For school systems the size of Cincinnati and Columbus, the dollars accrued from a single day of state aid allocation are considerable.

The Columbus school system undertook to receive maximum reimbursement and created a masterful document. The first part was designed to insure that all fifteen days of emergency legislation were counted. Through correspondence starting on February and ending in May 1977,[17] Columbus officials convinced State Department of Education personnel to count (a) three days when schools were closed prior to passage of emergency legislation (January 28, 31, February 1), (b) three days for the one day per week of school with schools that occurred between February 7 and February 25, and (c) nine other days to count for "equivalent" School Without Schools activities that had occurred February 5-25. The rationalization for the out-of-school activities had to be calculated in terms of conventional requirements for minimum hours to "make" a school day. The following rationale, complete with supporting figures and formula for calculation, was presented to the state department:

> Principal reports of activities show that there were 87,704 pupil instructional contacts during the first week; 90,099 in the second week; and 89,638 in the final week, including building-scheduled field trips, tutoring, small-group instruction, and home visits.

> Centrally scheduled field trips provided instructional opportunities for an additional 99,697 pupils throughout the three-week period.

> Small-group instruction was available to pupils in more than 1,000 community-provided facilities, including churches, businesses, recreation centers, private homes, and colleges and universities.

At the secondary level, there were 45 total hours of TV programming offered (daily average, 3.00 hours) and 52.50 total hours of radio programming (daily average, 3.50 hours). At the elementary level, there were 51.25 hours of TV programming (daily average, 3.41 hours) and 71.25 hours of radio programming (daily average, 4.75 hours). We believe that the above information supports our request for additional days of credit. We would, of course, be pleased to meet with you to discuss this request at your convenience. We await your consideration.[18]

On May 11, 1977, the state superintendent granted Columbus schools fifteen days' reimbursement, all under the legislature-provided rationale of lacking fuel.

However, the creative rationalization of Columbus schools was not finished. In separate correspondence, the state department had also granted Columbus reimbursement three other days (called "weather days"). The schools were closed during winter 1977 (January 10, 11, 18). In total, Columbus city schools received state reimbursement for emergency options taken during eighteen days of the 1976-77 school year.

In contrast, Cincinnati prided itself on the ability to retain (and rationalize) normal school operations in the face of crisis. A clear distriction was made between those winter days when the system closed down completely and those days when transportation was lacking. In sum, Cincinnati schools could claim only seven days for emergency state reimbursement.[19] The conscious effort to limit the impact of crisis to portions of the total school system hindered assessment by SDE, which tended to judge compensation on an either-or basis.

In summary, decision relationships between the SDE and two school systems revealed considerable variation in recognition of appropriate crisis response. Columbus was able to present a successful case for complete compensation while much of the Cincinnati effort went unrewarded. One reason may be the geographic location and visibility of Columbus schools *vis-à-vis* Cincinnati. However, the general reason cited in relation to qualifying for SDE compensation was the partial or complete effort to adjust to winter crisis.

Conclusions

Based upon the specific decision activities involving natural gas supplies, pupil transportation, existing personnel agreements, and compensation from SDE, several inferences can be made about system-wide differences in Columbus and Cincinnati's planning in a time of crisis.

The resolution of specific decision issues followed the larger format of whether crisis adaptation was to be a carefully planned new organization or an ad hoc compensatory adjustment. However, specific decisions added critical details about system-wide variations in crisis response. For example, the larger decision to close all local schools or a small number of schools had direct implications for the decisions about energy conservation. Columbus officials could rely on custodians and building engineers to maintain the mothball conditions of closed facilities while Cincinnati officials had to attempt to persuade occupants of buildings to practice personal conservation.

A second finding related to fuel conversion efforts was that the older facilities of Cincinnati were more likely to contain multiple heating systems than the newer buildings in Columbus. Modern fuel systems, such as natural gas or electricity, were more likely to be the exclusive means for heating of newer schools. Older facilities were more likely to be heated by coal or oil. When natural gas was added to the older facilities the other heating was deactivated but not removed. Conversion of these conditions was much easier and faster than adding totally new systems. Consequently, Cincinnati officials were able to incorporate the option of fuel conversion in overall adaptation efforts to a greater degree than Columbus planners.

A third finding was illustrated by decisions concerning the season carryover of natural gas and the pooling of base allocation amounts of natural gas for local schools. Allocation of gas supplies was a different policy issue than actual availability. Until winter 1977 the primary assumption of fuel supply was presented as an issue of base allocation. However, study of how aggregate supplies of gas were actually judged showed that availability could be adjusted by specific mechanisms of "creative accounting." The planning of natural gas supplies for both school systems was presented as use patterns and demands *vis-à-vis* the original base allocation and subsequent curtailment imposed by local public utility. However, the realities of specific decisions concerning actual fuel available to heat facilities showed other considerations. The impact on policy planning was to create two worlds of securing natural gas, "what we say and what we do."

Decisions about pupil transportation showed the benefits of incorporating this problem as part of a larger planning effort rather than attempting to adjust on a day-to-day basis. Special pupil transportation services were critical to implement School Without Schools and Cincinnati's host-guest arrangements. Columbus made decisions in this area, utilizing a full-time team of seven administrators, while Cincinnati relied on one full-time person and several other administrators that became involved on an emergency basis.

Finally, the two systems differed in their presentation of emergency actions taken during winter 1977. From the outset, Columbus declared the winter conditions "unique and unprecedented" to rationalize total system adaptation. Cincinnati described their adaptation efforts taken during winter 1977 as a modification of normal operations. The result of the two types of presentation was related to the extent of extra compensation given to the systems by the State Department of Education. Because Columbus was able to show a total adaptive effort taken, the case for "real emergency" (and need for extra compensation) was legitimized.

The variations of response to actual decision-making issues that had system-wide implications were mirrored by other choice variations which occurred at local schools. We now turn to local school decisions and planning which revealed organizational variation in winter 1977.

Notes

1. In some cases outside furnace dampers were closed completely, in violation of local and state health codes.

2. Cincinnati and Columbus schools provided extensive directions for moth-balling facilities because they were able to draw upon materials provided by the State Department of Education. After the Xenia tornado tragedy in 1974, Ohio education officials were directed by the governor to provide outlines for emergency adaptation of facilities. These directions formed the basis of mothball instructions given by both school districts in winter 1977.

3. The suspicion that personal conservation was not necessary to alleviate 1977 shortages was voiced by teachers in four sample schools. Another violation of energy efficiency was the teacher's use of a personal space heater (electrical) under his or her desk.

4. Beyond the classification of industrial and commercial user, there is also a distinction between *end use*, which considers type of use (for example, firing boilers, heat treatments) and *pro rata*, which classifies by whole categories. It is possible for a school system to be classified under *both* end use and pro rata classifications in a particular utility's priority system of availability and curtailment.

5. *Interim Order*, P.U.C.O. Case No. 75-548-GA-AGC, filed June 20, 1975; approved October 31, 1975.

6. The policy implication of self-help gas proved to be more a valuable documentation of the decision maze surrounding natural gas allocation rather than any energy relief. The final amount received by the Columbus schools was 59,500 MCFs. Further, the amount paid for the gas (approximately $2.90 per MCF) made a large-scale venture prohibitive for school users.

7. Letter from Campbell to Couzins, February 18, 1977. Actual additional costs for pupil transportation during the emergency are not as simple to calculate as presented here. For example, the Cincinnati schools were able to suspend a contracted reimbursement with Metro transportation for months in winter 1977 with "inclement weather" days. This "saved" the schools over $100,000 in fixed costs.

8. Letter from David Campbell to Jerome Couzins, February 18, 1977. The Columbus schools did receive $25,000 from the municipal government and other Title XX funds from emergency legislation HB176 (passed February 17,1977) to cover field trip expenses taken as part of School Without Schools.

9. *Collective Bargaining Contract*, Cincinnati Board of Education and Cincinnati Federation of Teachers, May 1977-December 31, 1979.

10. Interview, November 10, 1977.

11. *Agreement between Columbus Board of Education and Columbus Education Association, September 1, 1976 to August 31, 1979* (hereafter *C.E.A. Agreement*), p. 62.

12. *School Without Schools Handbook* (Columbus: Columbus Public Schools, February 2, 1977), p. A-5.

13. The *C.E.A. Voice* 7:22(February 1, 1977).

14. Ibid., 7:27(February 21, 1977).

15. It is interesting to note that the O.A.P.S.E. master contract recognizes the possibility of Interim Negotiations only for a change in state law "which would invalidate any provision of this Agreement." This is probably why the O.A.P.S.E. Memorandum is in the form of an administrative agreement, rather than Board-ratified policy. See *Agreement between Columbus Board of Education and Ohio Association of Public School Employees—Columbus Public School Chapter—Effective July 1, 1977, Article XVIII* (hereafter *O.A.P.S.E. Agreement*), p. 58.

16. Senate Bills 51 and 156.

17. Between Edwin Tilton of Columbus schools and James Lantz and David Long of the State Department of Education. The original correspondence confirmed the days as reimbursable. Tilton to Long, May 6, 1977; Walters to Tilton, May 11, 1977.

18. Dr. Lantz, SDE, judged that three days during the February 7-25 period could be counted as school in session "since each of our schools held one full day of school each of the three weeks during that period." Memo from Edwin Tilton to David Long, May 6, 1977. To compute field trip activities a standard hour per student was calculated for actual students and hours in field trips to various locations. This was then divided into the total Columbus enrollment (assumed to be 96,000) to create a standard hours per student figure. This figure was divided by 4.5 hours (to equal a minimum school day) and the result was an "equivalent" school day figure.

19. Cincinnati did claim three days when the total system was closed. In addition, four other days were claimed by the combining of half day shifts. See note 8 of chapter 2 for details.

Local School Planning and Decision-making

Another source of intraorganizational variation was the specific plans and decisions made by those who occupied local school sites during winter 1977. To this point, the adaptation taken by the school systems has been discussed according to the extent of governmental rearrangement which could be attributed to the winter crisis. Columbus's School Without Schools plan closed all but certain cluster schools to carry out instructional activities. Further, the cluster school sites were shared by the pupils, teachers, and principals of the other closed schools so that one day of normal class activities could be conducted each school week. It was shown that the Columbus central office provided numerous services to the local schools during the crisis including television and radio programming, bus transportation, food service, and athletics. Finally, it was noted that the School Without Schools plan called for extreme decentralization in both the governance of cluster school sites and the actual instructional and curricular activities to be conducted during the month of February 1977. Principals of closed local schools and their designated cluster schools made joint decisions about the scheduling of classroom space, coordination of bus transportation needs with the central office, and other governance activities (for example, mail and health services were coordinated at each cluster). One of the findings about the School Without Schools effort was the perceived success of the cluster administration by the principals involved.

The Cincinnati adaptation effort was described as attempting to minimize the extent of crisis rearrangement to school governance and to replicate normal operations throughout February 1977. Major areas of crisis modification included the provision of pupil transportation and the host-guest pairing plan which closed large user natural gas schools and placed their occupants in other facilities.[1] Governance of local schools was to imitate noncrisis conditions to the fullest extent possible.

Within the general outline of governmental arrangements for Columbus and Cincinnati there is a vast area of intraorganizational variation (perhaps the greatest source of difference in the entire adaptation phenomenon). This source is the collective plans and decisions made by individual principals, teachers, and custodians during the winter 1977 crisis. Regardless of central office and local school governments in either school system, the implicit assumption of actual crisis operation rested with individuals at the classroom level. In Columbus, the recognition of individual decisions and planning as the largest source of intraorganizational variation was expressed inferentially in the aggregate statistics explaining

School Without Schools efforts (for example, publicity releases and formal reports noting the participation of students in field trips). What was not presented in formal documents was a sense of how individual teachers and principals actually participated in educational activities.

In Cincinnati the replication of normal operations infers the intraorganizational variation of deciding and planning at the classroom and individual teacher level. As we shall see, this recognition was less public but just as pronounced in Cincinnati discussions of actual operations during the 1977 winter.

The primary data base for making judgments about individual planning and deciding during the 1977 winter was the sample of teachers, principals, and students which occupied the twenty-one local schools serving as case studies for this research.[2] Generalizations about the decision roles of administrator, teacher, and other local school occupants were, obviously, not exhaustive of all local decisions but served only as primitive yardsticks of actual patterns of variation. It is interesting to note, however, that findings derived from this methodology were, essentially, consistent with results of another study that sampled individuals from the populations of local school incumbents (that is, a random sample of all teachers) in Columbus.[3] What this study added was the relation of incumbent perceptions about crisis adaptation efforts to the particular local school locations where adaptation occurred during winter 1977.

Format for Autonomy

A major finding of this study was the extent of actual decision autonomy given to the classroom teacher in Columbus and Cincinnati during the crisis period. In Columbus schools the teacher responsibility for personal initiative was transmitted in the School Without Schools *Handbook* under directions for attendance and grades:

1. Pupil attendance is required and teachers must record attendance for *assigned school days. Assigned school days include those days when the school is in session,* whether one day a week or as many as five days a week in a Columbus Public School facility or another approved facility.

2. Credit shall be awarded to students for participation in the "School Without Schools" program. *Teachers should be advised to use the same techniques that they use in their regular school program to assess grades and to award credit for the completion of school assignments and approved projects.*

3. *Teachers are not required to maintain or submit to the principal a log of activities.* (emphasis added)[4]

It was clear from the beginning that the 1977 winter posed special conditions which made the continuation of the regular school program impossible. Curriculums and instructional activities involving special equipment or facilities (for example, chemistry laboratory) could not operate normally when the school site was mothballed. Administrative directions for the actual methods of achieving normalcy were not forthcoming from the Columbus central office or cluster levels of emergency government. The Columbus administration made it clear that there would be *no* evaluation of actual teaching-learning processes which occurred during February 1977. On February 2, the superintendent of schools further emphasized that there would be no required description of actual teaching processes:

> Each teacher will continue to be responsible for his/her pupils every day. Attendance will be taken at scheduled activities and grades will be assigned on the basis of work completed and handed in. Beyond that, we are taking a "common sense" approach to education, relying on the ingenuity and the creativity of our staff. The safety, health and welfare of students will be our primary consideration at all times.[5]

In spite of these statements some reporting of teacher activities did remain a necessity. Columbus officials knew at the outset that records of attendance and pupil grades would be primary evidence to substantiate the claim that education occurred during School Without Schools. When the Ohio legislature provided the opportunity to receive emergency compensation the need to gather additional evidence of education occurring under unusual circumstances became critical. The reporting of grades and attendance would be required of all Ohio school districts but the SDE would have special interest in the Columbus schools' justification of four days a week spent in alternative activities.

There was little hope that a simple statement supporting the autonomy of individual teachers to decide worthwhile alternatives based upon "creativity and ingenuity" would suffice. Some of the evidence deemed critical to support the case that Columbus schools were, in fact, educating pupils under special arrangements meant obtaining the activity information only individual teachers could give. The major controversy of School Without Schools concerned first whether individual teachers had to report actual activities and, second, if so, what was to be reported and to whom.[6] It was noted earlier that the Columbus teacher federation was involved from the outset in all planning and major decisions concerning School Without Schools. This central office arrangement allowed the resolution of what could have become an impasse. Consideration of the issue revealed that teachers were not concerned about reporting specific activities per se, but were concerned (particularly in certain local schools) that they would report to their principal.[7] Once the teachers were convinced that information would be collected at the central office and would only be used to present aggregate summary data, the seeming controversy between reporting and not reporting was resolved. Once resolved, the actual information collected and reported to the SDE to substantiate education during School Without Schools far exceeded scrutiny of the teaching-learning process in normal conditions. Summary data were presented by week and by day for the following: (1) numbers of students and teachers involved in field trips, tutoring, small group instruction, use of telephone or home visit; (2) number and type of nonschool facilities used for instruction; (3) specific field trip activities by type of program, community organization affected, and grade level of students involved; (4) use of media instructional time. When these data were presented to SDE[8] with student attendance and grades, the Columbus school rationale made an impressive, well-documented case for compensation.

In Cincinnati, establishing the format for individual autonomy in deciding crisis activities was less direct than in Columbus. The first evidence that teachers would be "on their own" arose in the issue of grading for the winter quarter. During January 1977 Cincinnati officials continued to operate on the assumption that school would be conducted under normal conditions. However, the number of missed days and problems with pupil transportation began to affect student attendance. Finally, on January 27, the following memorandum was given to all teachers:

> *Grading Procedures*—Erratic pupil attendance for the past few weeks necessitates an alteration of grading procedures for the second quarter.
>
> The special provisions are as follows:
>
> 1. Excused absences will not adversely affect a pupil's grade.
> 2. The second quarter report card grade will reflect performance *only* for those days on which a pupil was present at school.
> 3. All pupils will receive a grade of A, B, C, D, or F unless work performed *on days present* was incomplete due to failure of pupils to accomplish assigned work on those days; in that case, a grade of "Inc." applies.
> 4. Known truants will be subject to the usual provision regarding the withholding of grades and credit.
> 5. Other complications are to be reconciled with the approval of the principal.[9]

This memorandum created some confusion among individual teachers and local school administrators (this was close to the peak of crisis for the Cincinnati school) and generated the following attempt at clarification five days later;

> Today (February 1) is the last day of the second quarter.
> We are adhering to today's quarter closing date for the following reasons:
>
> 1. It has already been altered once.

2. Further delay would encroach upon an already uncertain third quarter.
3. Curtailment of additional school days may occur in the immediate future.

Needless to say, erratic pupil attendance for the past few weeks necessitates some alterations of grading procedures for the second quarter. The following provisions need to be emphasized.

1. *Excused* absences will not adversely affect a pupil's grade
2. The second quarter report card grade will reflect performance *only* for those days on which a pupil was present at school.
3. All pupils will receive a grade of A, B, C, D, or F *unless* work performed *on days present* was incomplete due to failure of pupils to accomplish assigned work on those days; in that case, a grade of "Inc." applies.
4. Arrangements regarding quarter examinations may be made at the option of the local school. One option available for this quarter only will be to waive examinations entirely and to base grades upon other work performed during the quarter.
5. Known truants will be subject to the usual provision regarding withholding of grades and credit.

In view of the varied circumstances we've experienced during the second quarter, and the resultant complications we *will* experience in assigning grades, it is important to note that principals will have the prerogative to reconcile with teachers matters not addressed by the arrangements previously cited.[10]

Although there was no further attempt to establish a format for emergency teaching roles, the implicit messages were clear. First, the burden for rationalizing grades given students for learning in crisis conditions would be the responsibility of the individual teacher and local principal. Second, there were few, if any, guidelines which could clearly establish "excused absences" or "known truancy" in January 1977.

Unlike Columbus, Cincinnati officials decided to take minimal advantage of possible SDE compensation (for example, only seven days of the possible fifteen "emergency days" legislated by the Ohio Senate and House). Student attendance and grades given by teachers were the only information solicited by the central office.[11]

Cincinnati Adaptations

The behaviors and perceptions of teachers and principals which occupied the twelve sample schools during winter 1977 allow some inferences concerning individual decision-making. There seemed to be some variation in the decision role of teacher or principal due to type of school organization for curriculum and whether the local school was part of the host-guest arrangement. The following cases serve as illustrations of the various local school situations.

Westwood Elementary

This school was illustrative of the majority of Cincinnati schools during 1977. It was elementary grades (K-6), a "neighborhood school" (in that no students were bused) and heated by coal. The Westwood school contained approximately 600 students, twenty-three teachers, and a principal.

None of the teacher respondents felt there was a crisis in winter 1977 as far as education for the children in this school. Specific questions about currinculum and instruction, student discipline and evaluation, and the role of the community and parents and administrators during January and February 1977 were answered in terms of normal operations.

The principal noted no direct effect of winter 1977 on the daily operations of the school, except that a temporary building had to be closed and students transferred to the main building. Although this move caused no complaint of student overcrowding, the abandoned facility sustained damage caused by freezing water pipes. The only suggestions the principal could make for future crisis adaptation was to maintain some heat in buildings that were closed (in the Westwood case no heat was turned on).

Kirby Road Elementary

This is another example of a local site unaffected by a crisis in winter 1977. Kirby Road housed somewhat more than 600 students in grades K-6. The school facility was an old building that was heated by oil. There were twenty-five teachers and a principal. No respondent felt there was a crisis for winter 1977. Teachers reported that all aspects of instruction and curriculum were unaffected.

The principal felt the Kirby Road school was untouched by winter 1977. She had offered the school as a guest site but the central office declined. Unlike Westwood, there was no mention of energy-related problems. Finally, the principal praised the central office for keeping the local school informed about the effect of winter 1977 on the total system but felt like it was a description of another world.

Rockdale and South Avondale Elementary

In contrast to the two previous cases, the Rockdale and South Avondale schools were involved in the host-guest student exchange and bore the brunt of crisis adaptation. Rockdale was a host school because of its multiple heating capacity (gas and oil) and its extreme underutilization (36 percent of capacity). The South Avondale school provided 300 student guests and nineteen teacher during the1977 winter. Even with these additional numbers, the facility would have been utilized at less than 70 percent (700 students in a 1,100 capacity) except that certain classrooms and temporary buildings were closed (those heated by gas). The result of closing parts of the building created what teacher respondents described as "overcrowding" and "cramped conditions."

The principal of Rockdale was described by teachers as a "go-getter who tackles a job without stopping for whys and wherefores." The guest South Avondale principal "was not pleased her school was closed and would not like to go through the experience again." However, she also felt "the host-guest was not the worst that could happen and definitely better than no school at all." The two principals shared responsibilities for administration.

As an illustration of the actual decision autonomy that occurred during winter 1977, the two principals decided to run combined classes from 9:00 a.m. to 3:15 p.m. rather than using the split-schedule arrangement stipulated by the central office. The staffs of both schools met for one day for orientation and preparation. A project member's notes[12] capture the specifics of curricular and instructional crisis modifications in the Rockdale site.

> . . . Arrangements were made for extra classes in a spare room, the supply room, the resource rooms, a faculty room, and the two stages. The librarian went "on wheels," the gym was partitioned, the learning disability classes were combined. Special education classes were tucked into landings and at the ends of halls. One spin-off benefit was a significant exchange of ideas among science, physical education and special education teachers as they worked together. The gym, science, art, and music rooms were utilized full-time instead of half-time. . . .

> . . . The instructional process really proceeded quite normally for the teachers who were in their "home" building. A day had been allotted for preparation, and supplies were shared with the "guests." Since the Northern Garage of the Board of Education is adjacent to Rockdale, additionally needed desks were easy to locate. . . .

> . . . The teaching problems all centered around three critical areas: absences, the effect of doubling classrooms, and restless students. Teachers experienced an inability to follow the regular curriculum and and inability to arrive at adequate evaluations. The students were excitable, academically disinterested, and harder to discipline.

Both the Rockdale and the South Avondale teachers who participated in the crisis adaptation effort confirmed the project member's observations. Absenteeism, use of halls, cold and doubled-up classrooms, lack of time, and lack of guides to evaluate students were common complaints. In addition, several teachers specifically charged the Cincinnati central office with being "too far removed to be of any real help" and indicated they felt abandoned. However, debriefing at the end of the host-guest arrangement revealed that teachers and administrators from both schools were proud of their abilities to "adapt, share and learn survival strategies to cope with winter 1977." The seeming contradiction between "feeling abandoned" yet being proud of abilities to "adapt and survive" may be explained as an orientation toward local decision-making. There were numerous expressions of confidence that adaptation to future crises was possible but that the responsibilities for action would not involve personnel outside the local site in any meaningful way.

Gamble Junior High

Gamble w as illustrative of junior high facilities involved in host-guest arrangements. As a coal heated school there was no shortage of fuel. However, in compliance with a central office directive all thermostats were set at 68° during school days and lowered to 35°-40° at night. A complaint among all teacher repondents at this site was that classrooms were too cold and that lowered temperatures affected student learning.

Gamble Junior High followed the central office directive of split sessions and made the transition to the host-guest arrangement by shortening each class, preferably by ten minutes. The school day for the Gamble Junior High staff and students ended at 1:00 p.m.; the staff and students from the host school then came in and the second session ran until 6:30 p.m. No additional arrangements were made except that additional public transportaiton was made available for staff and students. There were no complaints about pupil transportation or the provision of school lunches.

The major problem identified in crisis adaptation was the high rate of pupil and teacher absenteeism. Student guests had a significantly higher rate of absence than home students. Teacher absenteeism created a special burden on the remaining teachers (increased numbers of students) because there were no substitute teachers available.

Both the principal and a majority of the teachers surveyed felt that the incidence of student discipline problems was significantly reduced during the crisis period. A majority of the teachers surveyed felt this was because so many "trouble" students were absent during this period.

The principal of Gamble identified three issues in the crisis adaptation effort. Foremost was the lack of comprehensive planning by central office and host-guest principals to anticipate administrative problems. The specific example of handling extra bus tokens for student transportation was cited as a "knee-jerk response." Second were the long hours of personal effort (12-16) required to make the host-guest arrangement work. Finally, the principal was most concerned that comprehensive student evaluation had been eliminated for the 1976-77 school year on the rationale of the "energy crisis" disruption.[13]

Western Hills Senior High

The final Cincinnati illustration was a host senior high that received guest students from a junior high. The Western Hills facility was heated by coal and oil and had a vocational annex that was heated electrically. Under normal conditions the senior high is utilized at more than 100 percent of pupil capacity.

Like all senior high schools in Cincinnati, many students rely on public transit systems or their own transportation. Approximately 50 percent of Western Hills students used the metro buses during the 1977 winter. Senior high administrators indicated that the central office gave them complete decision autonomy in curriculum and instruction matters during the crisis. Their major concern was the mandated thermostat controls, especially the directive of lowering night-time temperatures to 35-40° .[14]

The split arrangement for dual use of the facility was described by the prinpal in the following manner:

> There was a 45-minute time period between Western Hills students leaving and Dater students arriving. There was a time strain on administrative personnel, as Western Hills people would arrive at 6:00 a.m. and study late until 3:30 p.m. and the Dater administrators would arrive early at 10:00 a.m. and then stay until 6:30 p.m. This same pressure was not on regular staff. The two administrative staffs got along fine and even built some friendships during the 45-minute noon period when they would meet to talk of common concerns. This extra admintration time in the building was not mandated by Central Office, but done in response to planning needs.

The split-schedule arrangement was perceived by staff and administration for use of the facilities worked as "working very smoothly." There were no special curriculum arrangements made for the crisis. Teacher respondents from the Western Hills staff commented that student absences, cold classrooms, and shortened teaching hours were the major problems for instruction. Student discipline and evaluation were not perceived as major issues to be associated with the crisis.

Conclusions

Although there is danger in overgeneralizing the study of operations in select sites to all local schools, some speculations can be drawn about variation in local decision-making. First, the issues perceived in winter 1977 seemed   different depending on the type of Cincinnati school at which one was located. Elementary schools were not affected by pupil transportation, food service, or (in non-host-guest situations) heating issues. Although host-guest participants were more likely to complain of coldness and overcrowding there were few effects to curriculum and instruction during the 1977 winter.[15]

The major issues cited at the junior high level were, in priority of perceived impact, student absences, extra teaching and administrative responsibilities, pupil transportation, and lack of comprehensive pupil evaluation. Student disci-line was perceived as improved because of the crisis due to novelty and that problem students stayed away. As with the elementary school, there was no direct modification of curriculum or instructional practices.

At the senior high level, transportation and pupil absence (although not at Western Hills) were the two issues related to local school operations affected by the 1977 winter. Normal classroom operations were not affected dramatically.

To address the question of the extent to which intraorganizational varia-tion of teacher and principal decisions were affected by the 1977 winter there must be two perspectives. First, classroom operations seemed to remain fairly normal regardless of type of school or whether a school was involved in the host-guest arrangement. This leads to the conclusion that the capacity to vary curricu-lar and instructional practices remained the same in winter 1977 as before or after.[16] Second, the total extent of normal variance in Cincinnati teacher and principal decision practices is unknown in any researchable format. Project efforts to ascertain general patterns of normalcy met with little success.[17] How-ever, in line with the intent of this study, the critical conclusion of lack of crisis impact on normal classroom (regardless of variation) practices remains the important finding. The Cincinnati school system attempted to maintain normal conditions in winter 1977, and at the individual teacher level of decision-making the attempt was generally successful. We now turn to Columbus schools.

Columbus Adaptations

Respondents from the Columbus local school sample perceived the winter crisis in two stages—preparing for School Without Schools and carrying it out. Unlike respondents from certain local schools in Cincinnati, all members of the Colum-bus sample felt winter 1977 was a period of crisis for education, and only one person questioned whether a crisis reorganization of the magnitude of School Without Schools was necessary. Most respondents argued that the weather and unavailability of natural gas in Columbus affected all local school situations in some manner and that there was no way to isolate this crisis to a subportion of the school system.

Northridge, Gettysburg, and Ohio Elementary

A composite of three sample schools suggests the type of decision experiences encountered in the most pervasive organization of local schools during School Without Schools; an elementary school housed within a cluster of elementary schools for the one day per week normal experience. Although the three schools share this characteristic, they differ in important ways such as the attendance of students during the crisis. Gettysburg elementary had better than 90 percent attendance throughout the crisis while Ohio elementary had less than 70 percent for the same period. Northridge varied between the two extremes.

When asked to explain the relation of pupil attendance to the winter 1977 crisis most respondents described normal differences among the three sites as the "real" reasons. Normal differences were described in terms of Gettysburg and Northridge's being small, new, highly utilized elementary schools in the suburbs while Ohio elementary was an old, large, but underutilized elementary school in the inner city. The "type of student" was cited most often as the reason for attendance, with some teacher respondents perceiving racial composition and extent of compensatory programs as "evidence" of why students attend or do not attend.

School Without Schools differences which could be related to winter crisis aspects of pupil attendance were most often decribed as issues of adapting to cluster school conditions and problems with securing bus services for field trips. Issues seemed to be emphasized by the particular cluster arrangement. Ohio and Northridge teachers had particular problems with pupil transportation, lack of classroom space in the cluster school, and lack of teaching supplies and materials. Gettysburg Elementary respondents emphasized the difficulty of teaching students familiar with a traditional self-contained classroom environment in a cluster school designed for open-space learning. Although it did not affect them directly, Gettysburg teachers noted the related problem of elementary students housed in junior or senior high schools serving as clusters. Specific issues cited for this arrangement were outsized desks and blackboards, lack of adequate playgrounds for recess, and older students' being inconsiderate of elementary pupils.

Perhaps due to the novel nature of School Without Schools, Columbus repondents were more willing and/or able to talk about specific administrative and teaching practices during winter 1977 than were their Cincinnati counterparts. Respondents in all three sample schools felt the one day per week in a cluster school was the best part of School Without Schools to reacquaint students, explain new work, and help with retaining skills in the basics of math and reading. Teachers were not impressed with field trips or television (particularly Gettysburg teachers) as adequate compensations for the face-to-face learning in a conventional classroom environment. As noted earlier, Ohio elementary teachers were disappointed by several aspects of sharing a cluster facility. Student attendance for class,[18] having to transport one's own teaching materials (due to lack of storage capacity in cluster and no prior planning to move supplies from closed to cluster facilities), and some teachers' "not pulling their share of the load" were cited by several respondents as problems of crisis cluster arrangements. There was no mention of problems with local school administration during the crisis from any sample school, although some Ohio and Northridge teachers felt the central office could have provided more guidance and coordination.

The *Handbook* was judged most helpful for crisis activities associated with closing the regular classrooms rather than providing guidance for activities during the one day per week classes. Several teachers said the *Handbook* helped in planning field trip activities but that they relied on other teachers and their principals in the actual selection and implementation of field trips. Respondents in all sample schools felt field trips were particularly worthwhile for elementary students (when transportation was available[19]).

Most respondents described the actual teaching-learning process during winter 1977 as most beneficial for the "slow learner needing remediation" because basic skills curriculum was emphasized.[20] Few described the field trips as integrated to the one day per week class activities. Of the faculty at the three schools, Gettysburg elementary teachers specifically mentioned the positive contributions of parents to supplement crisis modification. On the other hand, several teachers in Ohio elementary cited the lack of parental support as the reason students did not attend school regularly. Finally, those subjects which involved special equipment or elaborate learning aids (for example, science or curriculums tied to use of audiovisual presentations) were modified the most during winter 1977. Without exception, modification meant suspension of modern curricular materials and instructional strategies to rely on traditional textbooks and teacher-centered presentations.[21]

None of the elementary school respondents felt a School Without Schools organization was preferable to regular school arrangements.[22] None wished to replicate the winter 1977 emergency organization, but if an energy crisis forced such a modification all teachers wanted more conventional classroom experience.

Alpine Elementary

Alpine elementary students used a nonschool facility during School Without Schools, and this represented a special case of emergency modification within the Columbus system. As pointed out in chapter 6 on local school governance arrangements, Alpine elementary was perceived as a special situation within the normal pattern of elementary schools (for example, high attendance, high achievement, high community involvement, and high percent of nonwhite students). It was one of the few local schools specifically pointed out by central office administrators as having an "extremely successful" experience during the 1977 winter.[23] One reason for success cited by Alpine elementary respondents was the fact that students met as classes five days each week of School Without Schools in a nonschool facility (church/community center). A second reason for success was the ability to retain the regular involvement of community help and the normal dynamic leadership of the principal during the crisis period. Most teacher references to emergency curriculum or instructional activities were prefaced with comparisons to the normal educational operations. The conclusion was that

School Without Schools was not too different from the regular school environment except that the opportunity for securing additional central office resources and supplemental activities (for example, field trips) was increased. Members of this school were the only respondents indicating a desire to replicate School Without Schools in the future. The general feeling was that a self-contained "community school" like Alpine elementary was likely to flourish regardless of the organization of the larger school system. The only concern registered by Alpine elementary respondents was that they retain their decision autonomy in any future emergencies.

Linmoor and Dominion Junior High

As was the case with the elementary sample schools, Linmoor and Dominion junior high schools were different in regular characteristics and in response to School Without Schools. Both schools were closed during February because they were large natural gas users. However, the regular building utilization of Dominion was over 80 percent, compared to 50 percent at Linmoor. The student body at Linmoor was 96 percent black and the school was tenth in all schools of the Columbus system in use of compensatory resources. On the other hand, Dominion junior high had a student body 89 percent white and very little compensatory resources (for example, title programs, special aids).

During School Without Schools, Linmoor students went to a senior high cluster school while Dominion students were housed in an elementary school. Over 90 percent of Dominion students attended school throughout School Without Schools while Linmoor student attendance had dropped below 70 percent by the third week.

Although there were some comments that could be related to the characteristics cited above (for example, "parents don't care" or "senior high students picked on junior high pupils") the general finding was the similarity of negative response to School Without Schools by respondents from both schools. Teachers in both schools mentioned problems with the cluster arrangement for the one day per week classes. Lack of space and materials, overcrowding in classrooms, problems in scheduling, inability to regulate heat (both "over" and "under" complaints), and teacher skepticism were cited by Linmoor and Dominion respondents. On the other side of the coin, there were no complaints from either school concerning transportation or field trips (other than lack of student attendance).

The actual conduct of teaching during the class one day per week emphasized lecture and teacher-directed discussion. There was an increased emphasis on written work and homework. Much of the classroom time was spent giving out assignments, taking up required work, and counseling "poor" students.[24] Students in both schools were perceived as better behaved than normal (a common feeling was that "troublemakers" stayed home), and discipline was not a major problem. All teachers described the learning that occurred as "basic" and "refresher."

Perhaps the greatest complaint of junior high respondents (echoed by senior high) was the confusion over student evaluation. There was a feeling that there was no administrative direction concerning the relation of student attendance to grading practices or whether grades during the emergency should be on pass/fail or considered as extra credit. These issues were never clarified, so pupil grades assigned during February 1977 varied teacher to teacher. One phenomenon that could not be explained by any Columbus respondent was the strong performance of pupils on standardized achievement tests given in spring 1977. The actual scores improved over the previous year. There were several teacher suggestions that students may have been motivated to "catch up after the School Without Schools vacation" or that the tests were invalid. No respondent related the emergency reorganization to student improvement.

Junior high and senior high respondents reported that television was used infrequently and radio or newspapers were used even less frequently as curricular supplements or replacements. None of the sample respondents took advantage of central office workshops designed to facilitate curricular or instructional modifications.

Although most teachers reported relief when School Without Schools was over, Dominion respondents were more adamant than Linmoor teachers in not wanting to repeat the emergency organization.

Brookhaven Senior High

Brookhaven senior high was closed during School Without Schools and the students met for the one day per week classes in another senior high cluster school. Brookhaven pupils registered a steady drop in attendance as February progressed (less than 70 percent by the third week), which was matched by a lessening of enthusiasm by teachers. Brookhaven is instructive because the respondents noted a difference of opinion between the beginning and last days of School Without Schools. The same problems of student attendance, overcrowding, and lack of materials and evaluation noted by the junior high teachers were repeated. However, the effort required to sustain emergency activities over time was particularly emphasized by the senior high teachers. Special problems of counseling students preparing for college, sustaining interscholastic athletic and extracurricular activities, and providing specialized or technical subjects (for example, chemistry, home economics, industrial arts) were related to the issue of sustaining operations over time. Lack of student interest was also related to looking forward to the early spring break.

As evidence of the desire of senior high respondents to not repeat School

Without Schools in its 1977 form, the largest responses to needed improvement were, first, mandatory student attendance and then adjusting conventional classroom experiences to "a minimum of two or three days per week." Teacher skepticism was perceived as the greatest issue of School Without Schools.

Conclusions

Variations in local school decision practices during the 1977 winter crisis seemed to follow some general patterns. First, there seemed to be some systematic difference by level of school organization. Elementary schools seemed better able to adjust to School Without Schools, perhaps due to a normal educational emphasis on self-contained classrooms and generalized subject presentation. Junior and senior high respondents seemed to have less positive experience with the major reorganization and were more prone to want specific guidance in planning and deciding (especially in the areas of pupil attendance and student evaluation).

The second major pattern was an attempt at the local school level to replicate conventional curriculum and instruction practices as much as possible. Most teachers perceived their role as emphasizing "the basics" and attempting to "minimize loss in student learning" during the emergency period. Only in the special case of Alpine Elementary was there an expression of positive, additional education opportunities associated with School Without Schools.

Third, there was a decision pattern which negated some of the most publicly touted aspects of School Without Schools. Although field trips were utilized extensively in instruction, television, radio, and newspapers were not. Those teachers who did indicate some attempt to incorporate media initially (either as substitute or supplement) discontinued their efforts.

Finally, there was some indication that local school decisions were made to "suffer the central office's reorganization as little as possible." Elementary school respondents felt more postitive than junior or senior high respondents toward School Without Schools, but the general sentiment was negative. Further, there was considerable skepticism as to whether such an emergency organization was needed, with some feeling it was a "central office ploy for publicity and extra resources." This skepticism, coupled with the expected temporariness of the emergency reorganization, tended to negate a true sense of "ownership." Teachers and principals participated by did not feel a part of the initial decision to implement School Without Schools or an inclination to try new practices during February.

With these conclusions about Cincinnati and Columbus variations in decision-making and planning at the local school level, the description of winter 1977 crisis adaptation is finished. We now turn to the practical and theoretical implications of what was found.

Notes

1. In actual implementation twenty-five of ninety-three Cincinnati schools were affected (fifteen closed schools into ten host schools). There was a larger plan available but not implemented in 1977 calling for sixty energy inefficient schools to be closed and their occupants to be housed in forty host schools.

2. See appendix B for methodological discussion.

3. See J.R. Sanders and D.L. Stufflebeam, *A Study of School Without Schools: The Columbus Ohio Public Schools during the Natural Gas Shortage, Winter 1977* (Kalamazoo, Mich.: Evaluation Center, Western Michigan University, 1977).

4. *Handbook.*

5. Open memorandum, Superintendent Ellis to Columbus personnel, February 2, 1977.

6. For example, the following statement was presented in the teacher federation newsletter:

> At its February 10 meeting, a sampling among the District Governors indicates that perhaps as many as half of the system's principals have not reproduced and distributed to their staffs the administration's memo (dated 2/4/77) which makes it perfectly clear that teachers are *not* to be *required* to keep logs of nor *report* their daily activities! It must be as frustrating to the Superintendent as it is to CEA that some principals either cannot or will not read or follow simple directions. Your Board of Governors asks that if your principal has not given you a copy of the memo which clearly states your reporting obligations that you politely ask him/her for your copy and report to CEA the kind of cooperation you receive.

CEA Voice 7:25 (February 14, 1977).

7. Interview, Assistant Superintendent for Instruction, October 14, 1977.

8. Letter to Lantz from Tilton with supporting documents, March 18, 1977.

9. Memorandum, Division of Curriculum and Instruction, January 27, 1977.

10. Televised presentation of Superintendent of Schools, February 1, 1977.

11. However, the basic issue in presenting the Cincinnati case to SDE for compensation involved how to rationalize the "shortened school day" of secondary pupils involved in host-guest arrangements. In Ohio, school day meant five hours of instructional activity for secondary pupils and four hours of activity for elementary pupils. The host-guest arrangement involved four-hour school days. The issue was resolved by counting four school days for every five days of host-guest operations involving secondary pupils (that is, adding up the hours of the percent of secondary students affected until they reached the total of a "regular school day" for all secondary students).

12. As explained in appendix B, each case study was conducted by an individual member of the research team. The notes represent a summary of personal interviews and on-site observations.

13. The Metropolitan Achievement Test is given to Cincinnati students during the winter. During the 1976-77 school year the test was not administered at all.

14. A water pipe burst on the windward side of a building (with the lowered temperature in force), causing considerable damage. The Western Hills principal and custodian had "warned the central office it would happen but were overridden." Note technical suggestion on page 37.

15. Several elementary school respondents saw no energy related reason for not giving system-wide examination but inferred the "real" reasons were "politically motivated" (for example, declining scores overall and especially in schools with 100 percent black pupils).

16. It could be argued that lack of system-wide testing even increased the capacity for variance during winter 1977.

17. Joining the good company of other teacher evaluation efforts which have had trouble creating general models of situationally specific phenomena.

18. Apparently there was some variation in attendance between the one day per week classes and the other days of alternative activities, but it could not be determined.

19. There seems to be a difference between actual and perceived unavailability of transportation. This varied from person to person, local school to local school, and local school to central office interpretation.

20. Several teachers and one principal said that central office administrators stressed emphasis of the use of homework and basic skill training during the crisis.

21. Some teachers just "suspended" the topic until the end of School Without Schools.

22. Northridge respondents were also concerned that reorganization efforts taken to respond to the energy crisis were superseded by later modifications to meet desegregation mandates. Specifically, Northridge, as a gas school, was closed in winter 1977 plans but mandated for use in Court-ordered desegregation planning which occurred in spring 1977.

23. Although this was not the sole criterion for sample inclusion.

24. Several teachers commented that their students who could not read well were "totally lost" during School Without Schools. However, Linmoor teachers also commented that pupils with the most learning disabilities were also the ones who were not in attendance during February.

Practical Implications

General Conclusions

From a practical standpoint, a concern with understanding the variations in the Columbus and Cincinnati school adaptations during winter 1977 centers on a single question: Why did one school system choose total reorganization in response to crisis and another did not? Superficial descriptors, such as being "big-city" school systems or being located in a "midwest, urban state" are not helpful. In-depth analysis of select environmental and organizational variables does provide a viable framework for probing the question. This study offers several general conclusions about the meaning of "winter crisis," based upon the 1977 experience.

What constitutes a winter crisis in school operations may not be a function of weather severity.

When the two months in 1977 are closely examined, the direct effects of weather severity pale in comparison with other factors which generated crisis in decision-making. It is true that winter 1977 was the harshest on record, being especially unprecedented when described by degree days or snowfall. Yet the extent to which weather conditions actually prevented pupil transportation in Cincinnati or made School Without Schools "imperative" for Columbus or damaged buildings in both school systems was minimal compared to other factors. For example, the Cincinnati description revealed that the issue of pupil transportation was also a function of interpreting insurance liabilities, of rescheduling existing bus routes, and of issuing extra tokens. School Without Schools was implemented because the existing promises of natural gas supplies by the public utility were not kept and because school officials had informal guarantees of compensatory resources from certain state agencies before reorganization.

It is significant to note that Cincinnati officials did not consider a total emergency reorganization necessary or expedient because their system had fewer facilities dependent upon natural gas and had better promises of available supplies from their utility. This also explains why Cincinnati had avoided serious discussions with either community agencies or state agencies likely to provide compensatory resources for dramatic action. In both Columbus and Cincinnati, the perception of crisis in 1977 was based more upon a "supply versus demand" assessment of the need to change than the actual severity of the weather.

Finally, much of the damage sustained to facilities in both school systems was more a function of human error in judgment and of a bureaucratic tendency toward standard solutions than of weather conditions. For example, Cincinnati central office officials mandated that night-time temperatures in school facilities be lowered to 35-40°. When local school administrators discovered ice on the inside of windward walls and requested raising the night-time temperatures, they were told to continue the stringent heat conservation measures. The resulting breakage of water pipes can be rationalized less as a case of deciders being undone by extraordinarily harsh conditons and more as a case of being "penny-wise but pound-foolish."

A Columbus example of the same bureaucratic tendency toward standard solutions, particularly in regard to weather-related issues, was the setting of local school thermostats at a single temperature. In modern, well-insulated, and energy-efficient buildings this practice made sense. In the realities of older, energy-inefficient facilities this practice resulted in radically uneven heating from classroom to classroom. Consequently, in certain facilities, windows were opened in some sections of the building while electric space heaters were used in others to compensate for the set standards.

The practical implication of *not* considering the winter crisis in terms of actual weather severity is to focus adaptive efforts on issues of organizational arrangement and human error in select decision practices. This study found that the operational meanings of "energy supply" and "rational adaptation" are a function of political understandings and calculations by key individuals. Further, a winter crisis is a phenomenon that often demands tolerance for varying conditions within the school system itself and an issue-to-issue decision posture. Efforts to establish standardized solutions (either in the name of rational planning or of bureaucratic efficiency) can be disruptive. The next discussion will point out the considerable differences between the assumptions undergirding long-range planning for energy crisis and those supporting short-range planning. This study suggests the need to maintain a short-range frame of reference during the actual emergency adaptation to a winter crisis.

What constitutes rational parameters for long-range planning about school adaptation before crisis may not be the same as the parameters established for short-range planning during crisis.

Whether the school system is engaged in long-range or short-range planning about energy concerns determines the very meaning of "energy problem." Table 9-1 presents specific differences in the decision foci of Cincinnati and Columbus planners when they were considering energy-related issues prior to winter 1977 and during the months of January and February 1977.

Table 9-1
Types of Energy Planning

Examples	Long-range	Short-range
I. General concerns	Fuel availability Cost increases	Weather conditions Overnight damage Mandated curtailment of fuel
II. Immediate issues	Determination of base allocation Retrofitting costs Conservation efforts	Bus operation Broken pipes Uneven heating of classrooms
III. Major decision actors	Central-office planners, educators, plant oper- tion and maintenance personnel, chief engineers	Local school principals, custodians
IV. Parameters of strategy	Week-to-week and/or "season"-to-"season"	School day to school day, day time to night time

Decision-making about energy is obviously delimited by four main factors: general concerns, immediate indicators that frame the problems, the identification of the major decision-makers, and the probable standard for judging "rational" strategy. An apt illustration of the distinction between long- and short-range planning could be elicited from the School Without Schools effort as it was envisioned in the latter part of January (and was exemplified in the *Handbook*, the creation of the central office operations center, and so on) and as it was perceived during implementation on some day in mid-February. But such information about distinctions in rational planning itself is neither surprising nor helpful from a practical perspective.

The problem is to determine how to handle the multiple planning rationalities with which a practitioner contends in making crisis decisions. This study suggests that a planner must consciously recognize that long-range determinations concerning energy crisis may bear little relationship to decision about energy made during crisis. Furthermore, rational, long-range decisions may look irrational in the throes of crisis. Thus, it is suggested that planning for energy problems encompass long- and short-range concerns simultaneously. It would also seem necessary, for the planning of long-range perspectives, to consider the difference between symbolic and operational objectives. Finally, analysis suggests that short-range planning concentrate upon "political criteria" rather than economic or legal indicators of rationality.

The Columbus and Cincinnati situations clearly reveal that long-range planning tends to be centralized and to be controlled by specialists. In contrast, most short-range decisions emanate from the "guys in the trenches." Mechanisms established to pursue long- and short-range planning concerns before crisis should mirror these natural divisions among the actual decision groups. Long-range planning task forces should resemble the Columbus Energy Crisis Committee in composition. Thus, the planning body would include: (a) technical experts in plant operation and maintenance; (b) representatives of the public employees' and teachers' federations (and local school administrators if they are so organized); (c) central office administrators responsible for internal, system-wide coordination of pertinent services (for example, pupil transportation, attendance, food services, and interscholastic athletics); and (d) central office administrators who are in linkage roles to key energy-related agencies in the school's environment. The actual size of this group depends upon how many individuals hold multiple roles and responsibilities, and how this mechanism is to be used (for example, general fact finding, actual decision body, court of appeal).

The utilization issue also raises the question of the function of the board of education members, if any, on this type of planning mechanism. In Columbus, board members served on the Energy Crisis Committee; but the role of that committee before winter 1977 consisted primarily of hearing technical reports on fuel consumption and of considering the relation of the school system to its public utility and certain state agencies. In late January 1977 some members of the committee were part of the ambitious effort to create the *Handbook*. However, during the actual implementation of School Without Schools the committee as a total body was relatively unimportant within the ongoing decision dynamics.

The inclusion of board members on an energy committee depends upon a carefully specified role for that long-range planning body and upon whether a board of education mechanism for considering energy-related concerns exists. A major finding of this study was that the 1977 crisis adaptation in both school systems was a professional decision-making process. Board members acted, in effect, either as the formal legitimizers for decisions already in force (although presented as alternatives or options) or as deciders about resources already committed. Those considering the composition of a long-range planning body should seriously consider the viability of a professionally dominated adaptation process, especially in the light of differences between symbolic and operational needs in a school organization facing a potential crisis. This study suggests that image is as important as action in decisions about appropriate long-range planning. Boards of education are responsible both for the image of leadership and the image of rationality in deciding about school matters (for example, boards are responsible for "policy formulation"). If board members do not have roles in long-range energy planning mechanisms, the board of education should have some specific, formal relation to such a body.

The short-range planning mechanism should be composed of different types of people (although linked together through the superintendent and the board) and should focus on different types of problems. This group would be much more a political strategy body, designed to consider issues which are part of the crisis dynamic itself (those problems of high personal threat and uncertainty and those issues where prior planning is not done). In Columbus a grievance procedure was instituted for teachers with problems but it was not used despite apparently deep, negative feelings about student evaluation, pupil attendance, and cooperation in the use of cluster buildings. The reasons cited for not using the grievance mechanism related to "lack of time" during the crisis and the feeling that the emergency itself was "a temporary and exceptional phenomenon" (and that formal complaints would be rationalized away on those grounds). A short-range planning group should isolate possible "hot issues" and consider how they could be alleviated during crisis conditions. Obviously, the issues will often be at the classroom level, relating to individual teacher concerns and to interpersonal problems. These by-products of an energy crisis must be faced squarely. Often the energy issues will simply offer a new format for endemic, normal problems of the school system.

The compostion of such a group would reflect those "in the trenches" and, therefore, those most likely to bear the brunt of political or interpersonal issues. This study identified three subsets of such individuals: (a) teachers, principals, and custodians from the local school; (b) central-office personnel responsible for dealing directly with individual teachers or principals on crisis issues (for example, the Columbus operations room personnel); and (c) central-office personnel coordinating the schools' interest with the community and energy-related external problems. Each subgroup needs to be represented in short-range political planning efforts. At a minimum, the efforts should include both a listing of hot issues and some alternative(s) for resolution, and the identification of key actor networks for crisis responses. The State Department of Education did not approve the Columbus compensation and deny the Cincinnati request—but select SDE officials did. A school system needs to identify such individuals and establish contact before a crisis. During the crisis it seems to be the political connection with key actors that guides decision-making rather than rational arguments based upon legal or economic arguments. Suspicions are alleviated or resources committed more often on personal trust than on elaborate documentation of costs and benefits or on who is formally related to whom in the hierarchy of legal authority.

In summary, what constitutes rational decisions before crisis may not be the same as what is considered rational during crisis. Schools should establish mechanisms for long-range and short-range planning of energy concerns. There should be open recognition that the nature of the energy problem, the composition of the planning mechanism, and the proposed actions for adaptation will differ dramatically between the long- and short-range planning bodies. Long-range planning should pay particular attention to symbolic and operational needs for decision action, and short-range planning should focus upon the ramifications of political and interpersonal concerns.

Adaptation decisions seem directly related both to the perceived threat to the organization and to the perceived availability of compensatory resources.

This has been a study of two school systems which had similar organizational characteristics and which faced the same weather conditions; yet Columbus adapted by major reorganization while Cincinnati opted for minimal adjustments. Three possible explanations for this variation in adaptation efforts relate to how deciders assess a crisis in general and to how a specific crisis threatens the existing organization and offers possibilities for compensation.

First, Columbus officials publicly declared and legitimized winter 1977 as a "true crisis" long before Cincinnati grudgingly admitted a state of emergency. In Columbus, the nature of the crisis was perceived as the natural gas shortage; that perception crystallized with the 50 percent curtailment of supplies on New Year's Day. This began formal recognition of a true crisis although the large-scale emergency adaptation was not implemented until a month later. In Cincinnati, the initial problem was not a natural gas shortage but pupil transportation difficulties. Since this issue was perceived as affecting only one-fourth of the students, it appeared to be "manageable with only some extra effort." In fact, the official school position (and many central office and local school personnel) failed to identify the entire 1977 winter with true crisis operations. Without the acknowledgment of crisis (whether justified or not) the school system would and/or could not consider major reorganization as a rational form of adaptation without the risk of being judged "overreactive."

The extent of threat to existing organizational arrangement seems to depend upon judgments made at the beginning of a crisis period and reassessments made toward the end of the crisis. The combination of curtailed gas supplies and the percentage of Columbus facilities totally dependent on natural gas contributed to a determination that the only options open to the system were to close or to adapt by major reorganization. Closing a school system the size of Columbus was viewed as a potentially costly undertaking (for example, loss in state aid based upon pupil membership and complex modification of existing contracts for personnel services).

Equally important (especially prior to the actual crisis) were the warnings by certain knowledgeable technicians in building maintenance that "closing a system" did not mean turning everything off. All facilities had to be maintained at certain critical heat levels or major structural damage would occur. Mothballing would involve the understanding and the cooperation of all custodians, administrators, and teachers; they needed to know how to prepare classrooms for closing, how to monitor the mothballed facilities, and how to reopen the inactive buildings. Ultimate cost and the difficulties of closure contributed to the decision to attempt a major reorganization. However, several Columbus officials interviewed felt that their school system would not have conducted educational activities in February 1977 if there had not been the promise of state and municipal compensatory resources for attempting the major reorganization.

The crucial decision to try School Without Schools was made between January 18 and 24. On January 16, the curtailment of natural gas was raised to 85 percent and the final evidence (that a true crisis was at hand) was available for those lobbying various state agencies. The governor's office, several key legislators, and SDE officials became convinced that Columbus schools faced a zero-sum (all or nothing) situation where the only hope for emergency relief was to secure promises of compensation for trying a radical venture. Columbus officials did not promise a dramatic example of emergency adaptation but indicated the willingness to try major reorganization if extra costs could be absorbed by the state.

In comparison with Columbus, the Cincinnati officials did not face an imminently critical situation due to natural gas shortage. On the first of January, the Cincinnati system was curtailed to a level equivalent to what had already been reached by voluntary conservation efforts (and equivalent to one-half the mandated level of curtailment under which Columbus schools had operated for two years). Dramatic curtailments (80 percent) were not imposed until January 28. Furthermore (and perhaps most important from a planning perspective), only one-eighth of the Cincinnati pupils were actually housed in large natural gas facilities. All of these internal factors contributed to the basic policy decision to minimize reorganization efforts.

Of significance, however, is the fact that Cincinnati also lacked an "inside track" in regard to knowledge of upcoming compensation possibilties from state sources. Cincinnati officials admitted that they had heard rumors of possible legislative actions in mid-January, but they did not know the details of such legislation until three days before the formal announcement. Perceptions of the absence of a total emergency and lack of awareness of emergency compensation avenues contributed to a utility-matching decision posture in Cincinnati. Reorganization decisions were based upon minimizing the losses of known, regular resources rather than risking massive organizational failure by relying on potential, but possibly illusory, compensations.

From a practical perspective, the crucial distinction for a school system debating the adoption of zero-sum or utility-matching postures in crisis adaptation seems to be a combination of perceived threat and compensation. Figure 9-1 presents a rough typology of these factors and hypothesized adaptation strategies. Obviously, the classification of Cincinnati as a Type IV situation is debatable (for example, when is one-eighth of a big-city school system a "small consequence"?); and the particular criteria for a utility-matching judgment will differ from decider to decider and from school system to school system in relation to the likelihood of attempting a major reorganization in the face of emergency conditions.

A word is needed about situations II and III. This research did not find these conditions in the school systems under study. Their actual existence in winter 1977 remains in the form of speculation generated by informal discussions with a number of Ohio administrators and board members after the winter crisis.

Expected Compensation

	Large	Small
Large	I	II
Small	III	IV

Adverse Effect on Existing Organization

CRISIS ADAPTATION STRATEGIES

I.   "Zero-sum" decision due to large consequences, large rewards (Columbus schools). Greatest likelihood of major reorganization.

II.   Large consequences, small rewards (a common perspective of many Ohio districts prior to emergency legislation). Greatest likelihood of total closing in face of emergency; same possibility of major reorganization.

III. Small consequences, large reward (a perspective of some Ohio districts not dependent upon natural gas after emergency legislation). Greatest likelihood of presenting an image of larger than actual consequences at time of requests for compensation.

IV.   Small consequences, small reward (Cincinnati schools). Least likelihood of major reorganization.

Figure 9-1. Typology of Decision-making in an Energy Emergency

Many local districts that were natural gas dependent in mid-January 1977 were considering a Type II decision. These were mostly modern suburban districts that served middle-class (not extremely affluent) communities. Type III conditions were rare, but actual situations with these characteristics existed after "emergency day" legislation was passed. The Type III prototype was the small, coal-dependent, rural district with close political ties to key SDE officials and legislators. There was one reported (but unconfirmed) case in which a local district "erased" a $400,000 operating cost deficit by gaining "windfall" compensation for emergency operations during the 1977 winter. Future research is needed to substantiate whether all four types of emergency adaptations exist in the real world.

In summary, three general conclusions can be drawn about the relationship between school system adaptation and a winter crisis. First, the criticality of winter crisis may not be related so much to severe weather conditions as to human factors associated with regular operating procedures. Second, the rationality of long-range planning which occurs before a winter crisis may be different from the rationality of short-range planning during a winter crisis. Finally, decisions about adaptation may be directly related to discrete combinations of perceived threat to the total organization and the possibility or available compensation for reorganization. From these general conclusions several practical implications emerge in regard to the specific types of adaptation attempted by the Cincinnati and Columbus schools.

Conclusions about Columbus

As an example of major reorganizational effort in an emergency situation, the Columbus case offers guidance both for the conduct of internal governance and decision-making, and for the conduct of relations in the school's external environment.

Internal Governance and Decision-making

Study of the Columbus school intraorganizational variation in crisis response focused upon central office arrangements, local school arrangements, and plans and procedures for adaptation. From a practical standpoint, the major finding concerning internal governance is that distinctly different meanings of "emergency reorganization" emerge when one studies system-wide indicators versus local school indicators of change.

The accurate description of type of crisis reorganization undertaken by the Columbus schools depends upon both system-wide *and* local school *perspectives.*

School Without Schools was implemented in winter 1977 by the Columbus Public Schools and was touted as an example of "major reorganization in the face of extreme crisis." This statement is true and not true, depending upon which view of adaptation a person takes. A system-wide, central office perspective of School Without Schools yields three conclusions: (1) the organizational effort was an example of innovative, planned change; (2) it affected the total system; and (3) it was a positive experience. A local school perspective of School Without Schools reveals an attempt to replicate conventional variation in effects on classroom behaviors and perceptions and a less positive experience.

The system-wide evidence for a description of major reorganization includes both information from technical and/or academic support services and guidelines (published and unpublished) for formal authority and responsibilities. A technical description would include such specific indicators as plant operations and maintenance of facilities in an internal fuel analysis of natural gas consumption (building by building) and directions for mothballing local school centers. The indicators of academic support services would include specialized functions which were centralized during the emergency: pupil transportation (for field trips); provision of food, health, media services, and athletics; and consolidation of student attendance data. Formal authority and responsibility guidelines would be deduced from the *Handbook*, the cluster arrangement of local school centers (a third tier), contract modifications, and the governance role of the crisis operations' center. All of the indicators suggested create one perspective of the major reorganization undertaken by Columbus schools in winter 1977. Select use of these types of indicators constituted the basic rationale for their emergency days compensation.

The local school view of the Columbus system during winter 1977 revolves around the perceptions and behaviors of individuals in the one-class-per week and four-days-per-week experience. The evidence of this view would stress actual processes of curriculum and instruction (for example, use of public media), interpersonal dynamics generated from the interaction of roles, and specific teaching-learning decisions. Issues of pupil evaluation, sharing classroom materials, and coping with thermostat settings reflect efforts to replicate conventional practices and to minimize the extent of crisis reorganization.

The distinction between system-wide and local school perceptions of what actually occurred in winter 1977 engenders two practical implications. First, the nature of the evidence shapes the image of crisis reorganization which can be presented. The Columbus study elucidates the types of information which can be collected and presented to highlight either perspective. Second, analysis of intraorganizational variation tends to find itself describing two opposite patterns of adaptation which occur simultaneously during crisis. The Columbus situation suggests that a portrait of intraorganizational variation will include both descriptions of the structural arrangements and the governance of specialized services, and indicators of the teaching-learning and interpersonal level of analysis. Further, the ability to distinguish "emergency" from "normal" patterns of intraorganizational variation will be greater in system-wide accounts of adaptation than in local school descriptions.

As a final note about the practical implications of internal governance during crisis, four observations about lasting impact or effect are worth recording. First, Columbus schools gained national recognition as an "innovative system" (and received extensive compensatory resources from state and community agencies) by emphasizing the "four-days-per-week" activities of School Without Schools. In contrast, the one basic agreement among central office and local school educators was the paramount value of having normal class one day per week. Second, in spite of considerable expressions of concern about reduced student learning and other adverse effects of February 1977 on teaching effectiveness there was no measurable indication in standardized test results that these fears were being realized. Third, the winter crisis of 1977 was quickly forgotten as the Columbus schools faced other crises inherent in the contemporary big-city issues of finance and desegregation. Finally, no organizational learning occurred which would allow Columbus officials to judge whether School Without Schools represented an appropriate contingency plan for future winter crises. The extra compensation secured, the image of being innovative and the negative opinion of teachers could all be judged simply as "novel expressions" of winter 1977 or as "likely occurrences" in similar adaptation efforts in the future.

Relation to External Environment

The decision arrangement between the Columbus school system and its external environment during the 1977 winter identifies two different patterns of relationship.

An accurate description of the type of "crisis reorganization" implemented by the Columbus system depends upon both symbolic *and* operational *interpretations.*

As the result of 1977 winter efforts, at least four symbolic impressions were conveyed to different audiences in the Columbus school environment. First, in the governor's office, the state legislature, the SDE, and many other Ohio school districts, Columbus became the "lighthouse model" of rational contingency planning for winter crises. Second, adaptation efforts of the Columbus schools were extolled for their "positive contribution" to the metropolitan area by individual governmental officials, members of the power structure, and the general citizenry. Third, Columbus schools cultivated the image of "knowledgeable leader" in educational energy issues through adroit maneuvers in regard to the allocation, regulation, and curtailment of natural gas, and the securing of additional supplies. Finally, Columbus administrators gained (or supplemented) a "proactive" image with their board of education and teacher federation for a perceived ability to govern in winter crises. Proactive meant the resolution of uncertainty to board members and the sharing of system-wide decisions to the teachers.

The operational pattern of Columbus school relations to the external environment reflects the specific outcomes of a favorable symbolic image. These outcomes are identified in (1) specific resources gained or lost as a result of reorganization, (2) the clear-cut linkages established with important decision bodies, and (3) the apparent autonomy of administrative control of reorganization decisions. Columbus schools gained considerable compensation for the 1977 effort both in terms of direct services during School Without Schools (for example, use of municipal buses and nonschool facilities) and in terms of assistance after the reorganization (for example, emergency days). Special linkages were established as a result of winter 1977; perhaps no other school district in Ohio enjoyed a greater influence role than that of Columbus school officials with public utility and state regulatory commission representatives, key state legislators, members of the governor's staff, municipal officials, and representatives of important community interest groups. Unlike other types of crises, the Columbus linkages for winter 1977 stressed mutual survival needs and produced an integrative form of decision relationship. These linkages were strong enough to override long-standing suspicions and competition among the various environmental groups. Finally, the central administration of the Columbus schools gained virtual autonomy for all major decisions about the nature of education during winter 1977. Because of the positive image associated with School Without Schools, the operational control for formulating and implementing policy in the reorganization was delegated willingly by the board of education.

The complex interrelationship of symbolic and concrete realities in describing how the system functioned in the crisis environment suggests that one prefaces the other. However, to hypothesize which is predominant or necessary for the other runs the practical risk of a chicken or the egg argument. The basic implication of this finding is the necessity of building both patterns of external relations for successful adaptation.

While Columbus represents a model of major reorganization in crisis adaptation, Cincinnati school essentially replicated normal arrangements during winter 1977. We now turn to the practical implications of that type of adaptation effort.

Conclusions about Cincinnati

A fundamental finding of the Cincinnati situation is that a big-city school system is unlikely to enter into major reorganization unless there is an acknowledgment of no other recourse for organizational survival. A premise of social systems theory is that all decision systems first ignore, then resist, and then adapt to stress to the minimum extent necessary for maintaining normal arrangements. The Cincinnati adaptation during winter 1977, as documented in earlier chapters, followed these theoretical steps toward systemic adaptation.

Internal Governance and Decision-making

Two major findings of the Cincinnati adaptation to winter 1977 emerge. First, crisis can be confined to a subsector of the total organization, and, second, a school system can replicate normal operations under unusual conditions.

Accurate description of the type of crisis adaptation adopted by the Cincinnati schools depends on understanding that success varied with the ability to limit crisis conditions to subsections of the total organization and the commitment by major deciders to operate normally.

This premise was sustained in the Columbus situation in that the perceived inability to limit crisis stimulated the effort to react in a novel fashion. In Cincinnati, on the other hand, there was consistency in central office and local school efforts to replicate conventional practices and minimize reorganization. Further, there was no discrepancy between the image of normalcy (for example, the superintendent's charge to close fewer days than any other Ohio district) and actual operations in most of the school system. Emergency efforts concentrated in pupil transportation, the subsector of host-guest schools, and the maintenance of facilities during nonschool hours. In these areas it is appropriate to discuss crisis adaptation, but in the bulk of Cincinnati school functions it was normalcy that prevailed.

However, even in the normal operations of the 1977 winter there were overall effects on school practices. At the system-wide level, the conversion of local schools to multiple heating systems received top priority when the possibility of fuel shortage became obvious. Second, standardized achievement testing was eliminated for the 1976-77 school year on the rationalization of the winter crisis. Third, all local schools lowered temperatures at night time as an emergency conservation effort.

In those twenty-five local schools that participated in the host-guest arrangement specific variations related to the 1977 winter occurred: for instance, special problems were detected in the areas of student grading and absences. Yet, in spite of conspicuous alterations, actual teacher practices in the classroom attempted to replicate conventional experience wherever possible.

Relation to External Environment

A noticeable facet of the relationship between the Cincinnati school system and its environment was the system's success in operating autonomously, eschewing the need for compensation or special recognition. Unlike Columbus, Cincinnati officials did not feel the threat of a natural gas shortage or the need for securing guarantees of help from state-level agencies. Instead of negotiating for compensation, officials in Cincinnati sought to minimize losses and "to make the best of a bad situation."

Summary

From a practical standpoint, the findings of winter 1977 suggest several avenues whereby educators may assess their own school systems or engage in comparative analysis. Variation in crisis response appears to be a function of the following factors:

1. Effect on total organization (fuel, facilities, transportation).
2. Compensation (state, local).
3. Long- and short-range planning parameters.
4. Weather.

Educators may wish to review energy decisions and conservation efforts made during the last part of the 1970s in order to give a rough self-estimate of efficacy. This study also implies that the priority of effect is reflected in the order of listing presented above and that major reorganization will only be attempted when the four factors offer no alternative for maintaining "normalcy."

Finally, the findings from Columbus and Cincinnati give guidance to the educator wishing simply to describe weather-oriented adaptations. Indicators of system-wide variation are found in the provision of specialized services (for example, food, transportation, health, athletics) and the alterations in formal arrangements (for example, master contract, emergency operations center). Local school indicators of variation are teacher behaviors in the conduct of regular teaching processes and the principal's role in governance (for example, extent of autonomy). A third indicator involves both the type of general image generated for the crisis period and the specific audiences targeted for symbolic presentations. The final set of indicators are comprised of the operational decisions concerning how to secure certain resources, the linking of schools to key actors in the external environment, and the autonomy to decide one's own fate.

These data should help the concerned educator deal with winter crises in a systematic and rational manner. The next chapter will explore theoretical implications of how this study relates to the existing literature on crisis and organizational adaptation.

10 Theoretical Implications

The results of the 1977 study offer more than practical advice to educators planning for winter crises which are caused by extreme weather or shortages of particular types of heating fuel. This information provides a means to assess several persistent conceptual issues of how crisis decisions are made in large organizations. The present theories of the bureaucracy and decision-making within an organizational context are in general agreement with the following premises:

a. The "rationality" of decision-making is a function of demonstrating consistency between a particular choice and the precedent of past decisions and/or the parameters of a projected future.

b. The "adaptive capacity" of a large bureaucracy is a function of the ability to reallocate "base" resources and/or the extent to which uncertainty can be avoided.

The following discussion elaborates upon the wide variety of opinions about how premises are actually realized in school systems and other types of large bureaucracies in contemporary society. However, despite these considerable variations, the general premises about "rationality" and "adaptive capacity" continue to persist. This study provides a data base to assess the two conceptual premises.

A third concept which this study addresses is the difference of opinion about how a crisis occurs in a decision situation. At present, the literature is divided as to whether crisis occurs as an evolution (" a gradual growth of doubt"), is revolutionary ("a sharp, disjointed breakthrough"), or whether phenomena exist conjointly. This chapter will seek to clarify the analytical meanings of the Columbus and the Cincinnati experience in relation to the concepts of "rational" decision-making, bureaucratic "adaptation," and "crisis."

Deciding in Large Organizations

There is an established body of literature which suggests that decision-making in large organizations follows certain patterns of governance and control. Furthermore, these actual patterns of deciding are different from the formal theories of bureaucracy and classic problem-solving. The formal theory of bureaucracy[1] assumes that decision tasks and choice relationships are fixed by formal rules,

131

formal rules, regulations, and standard operating procedures. These components will inevitably lead to the achievement of total bureaucratic purpose. Key dimensions of the bureaucracy include: hierarchy of centralized authority in a line and staff, "span of control," which ties together the specialization and functional differentiation among decision roles, and strict control over any disruptive "inputs" from the external environment.[2]

Classic problem-solving has been described by Dror[3] as "pure" rationality. This process assumes six phases which are followed in making a decision:

a. Establishing a complete set of operation goals, with relative weights allocated to the different degrees to which each may be achieved.
b. Establishing a complete inventory of other values and of resources, with relative weights.
c. Preparing a complete set of the alternative policies open to the policymaker.
d. Preparing a complete set of valid predictions of the costs and benefits of each alternative, including the extent to which each will achieve the various operational goals, consume resources, and realize or impair other values.
e. Calculating the net expectation for each alternative by multiplying the probability of each benefit and cost for each alternative by the utility of each, and calculating the net benefit (or cost) in utility units.
f. Comparing the net expectations and identifying the alternative (or alternatives, if two or more are equally good) with the highest net expectation.

While most prevailing theories of decision-making identify some variation from the classic model, Dror and others[4] argue that the essential assumptions remain.

In contrast to these discussions of bureaucratic theory or classic decision-making there are concepts of how organizational decisions occur which are based upon actual practice.[5] The patterns of choice which are described by this body of literature emphasize the "bounded"[6] nature of rationality and the "informal" bureaucracy. Bureaucratic organizations govern and decide in a "marble cake" fashion, where people "networks" and "regimes" of vested interests modify the clear-cut "layer-cake" hierarchy of formal authority and responsibility. The combination of the human capacities for calculation and the dynamics of organizational size and complexity create the following realities[7] of decision-making:

a. Large crisis problems will be divided ("factored") into various subunits of the total organization so that stress can be shared ("decomposed").

Under this assumption Cincinnati and Columbus schools would be expected to spread the impact of winter 1977 among various subunits of the total organization (for example, local schools) rather than to attempt to face the problem in a centralized manner. At the operational level, the decision of stress to local school, classroom, and individual educators did indeed occur in each school system. However, it is important to note that both organizations attempted also to retain the image of system-wide problem-solving and a centralized response in select specialized services.

b. Organizations are limited in the extent of actual change which can occur in response to crisis by fixed patterns of allocated resources and the tendency to negotiate decisions toward maintenance of the status quo.

This statement suggests that Columbus and Cincinnati could and would make only minimal adaptations to the unusual conditions of the 1977 winter. Much of the popular literature about large organizations emphasizes that the capacity of deciders to make purposive change is very limited, both by the dynamics of the bureaucracy itself and by the precedent of past decisions. (Some argue that only a "marginal" adjustment of less than 5 percent of the total allocation is possible at any one time.) A second strain of the literature suggests that, beyond the "natural" limit of change capacity, there is a tendency for bureaucrats to be "conservative" and to orient decisions toward maintenance of the status quo.

The Cincinnati experience seems to confirm these predictions exactly. Certainly, the major decision-makers of the central office and the local school personnel who were interviewed did not question the need to replicate "normal operations" wherever possible. The actual pattern of resource reallocation which was adjusted due to winter 1977 was small in comparison to the total base. Examples of major change were limited to specialized services (pupil transportation) or certain subunits (host-guest schools) of the organization. Because formal personnel practices continued unaltered, because most local schools operated untouched, and because the system felt no real need to secure external compensation, the marginal argument is sustained in this case.

Superficial analysis of the Columbus adaptation efforts seems to cast doubt upon portions of this theoretical conclusion. The central office educators were committed to a "radical alternative" and not to maintain the status quo during the winter crises. However, this was only decided after guarantees for extra-effort compensation were realized. In spite of the dramatic evidence of new curricular and instructional options (for example, field trips, television, and radio), and new local school organization (cluster), an economic interpretation of actual adjustment to the original base allocation would still use the term "marginal." Although an exact accounting of all extra costs incurred during February 1977 and all extra compensations received for emergency actions was not possible, there is some reason to speculate that Columbus gained in total resources and did not disrupt the base allocation of the bureaucracy at all.

A second consideration about the actual extent of change which occurred in Columbus during winter 1977 was the mindset of teachers and principals at the local school level. Certainly the four days a week without a classroom and the cluster arrangement for shared facilities forced new teaching-learning processes.

This suggests that the bureaucracy did change dramatically during School Without Schools. However, this study found that local school teaching personnel preferred normal conditions and attempted to replicate conventional practices whenever possible. This finding seems to support the "tendency toward the status quo" premise.

c. Organizational decision-making in crisis will emphasize "short-run" problem solving over "long-run" strategies, "groupthink" for interpersonal cohesion, and, under extreme stress, "calculated inactivity."

This proposition is based upon Allison's findings about organizational behaviors in the face of crisis (for example, the presidential cabinet and the 1962 Cuban missile crisis) and psychological literature about the way individuals and groups cope with stress.[8] The underlying premise of all three indicators of deciding in crisis is the compelling need to circumvent the feeling of uncertainty. The organizational literature suggest a preoccupation with uncertainty avoidance, for ambiguity in choice is assumed to be "risk." Allison argues that the first line of defense against uncertainty is to arrange a stable, negotiated environment with standard scenarios prepared for uncertain contingencies.[9] However, the final processes of crisis decision-making (if the defense fails) occur in the "situation-oriented" arena of key actor bargaining.[10]

A second form of uncertainty avoidance found in bureaucracies under crisis conditions is what Janis coined "groupthink."[11] Conformity mandates, necessary for small-group cohesion under stress demands, lead individual deciders to create the shared illusion of invulnerability through unanimity. Groupthink is characterized by "global and undifferentiated thinking, dichotomized modes of thought, oversimplified notions of causation, loss of sense of proportion, and confusion of means with ends."[12]

How a crisis situation reaches the proportions where a collection of individuals value the security of "psychological huddle" over consideration of calculative choice is still uncertain.[13] It has been suggested that "the relation between intensity of fear arousal and adaptive coping responses is *an inverted U-shaped curve.* Moderate fear arousal . . . acts as an emotional inoculation enabling normal persons to increase their tolerance for stress"[14] (emphasis added). Under extreme fear conditions, an extension of the groupthink literature would seem to infer a peak period of groupthink and then a posture of nondecision. This posture might be analogous to the description of Coolidge's "calculated inactivity." The strategy is to "sit down and keep still . . . to remain silent until an issue is reduced. . . ."[15]

The decision behavior of Cincinnati and Columbus officials in early January 1977 suggests that the general premise was partially substantiated. The "negotiated environment" (long-range plans) and emergency scenarios for maintaining enough natural gas or for transporting pupils were quickly outstripped, and both systems reverted to key-actor bargaining to make decisions. These actors reflected facets of the crisis situation rather than official organizational positions (with the exception of the superintendent).

The groupthink and calculated inactivity arguments are harder to identify in either school system. Once the unusual conditions of winter 1977 became known, officials in Columbus and Cincinnati acted decisively (although toward different objectives). It could be argued that the early discussions of School Without Schools or host-guest arrangements had some groupthink characterist-tics, but these were not evidenced in actual implementation efforts. Further, both systems seemed more inclined to take some resolute action ("act normally" or "to change dramatically") than sit still.

d.   Adaptation activities undertaken in crisis will be replaced with normal gov-
     ernance arrangements as soon as conventional decision parameters can be
     reestablished.

General systems theory speculates that all social organizations change as a result of tension from the environment. The tension comes from the stress created either by demands for refinement of existing systems arrangements or by demands for a new form to replace the existing organization. The organization will survive by adapting to the degree necessary to alleviate stress and to main-tain equilibrium. For this study, the type of equilibrium a school system could achieve in response to the stress of the 1977 winter was important. There is a distinction between a dynamic equilibrium (called "steady state"), where an organization alleviates stress by creating a balance in movement (for example, the person running forward) and a static equilibrium, where stress is alleviated by achieving a stationary balance (for example, the person standing still). Orga-nizational literature suggests that static equilibrium is more likely in large bureau-cracies.[16] The Cincinnati and Columbus experiences both seem to support the "standing still" reaction to demands for change. In the local schools of both sys-tems the behaviors and the preferences of the teachers indicated a desire to return to normal. Even in Columbus, with the much-publicized image of a radi-cal change effort, the teachers perceived 1977 winter conditions as a temporary phenomenon and believed that change from conventional practices would stop when the crisis was over. This study found no one that expected the differences in practice caused by the winter to continue after the stress of crisis disappeared.

Another reason why both Columbus and Cincinnati demonstrated a static equilibrium in adapting to the winter crisis was the advent of other stress demands for change in the spring of 1977. Further, these spring crises were more familiar and endemic to the school systems over time (for example, finances, desegregation, teacher strikes), while weather crisis retained the image of being unique and a "one-shot" affair. In spite of the enormous amount of information to the contrary, a significant number of participants in this study either believed that the natural gas shortage was a hoax or that the 1977 weather conditions could not occur again.

A final reason why the schools reverted to governance arrangements that imitated prewinter 1977 conditions was the need to rationalize the organization's performance to state-wide agencies. Legal statutes and regulations which describe public schooling in the state predicate a fixed picture of the educational organization. Further, those who inhabit state-level bureaucracies and are responsible for justifying change modifications demand presentations which utilize the conventional format. The Columbus experience shows that the most radical adjustment to stress can be justified *ex post facto* as normal schooling, but the experience also shows that justification is keyed to a conventional format and understanding of what public education is.

In summary, four theoretical conclusions about decison-making in large organizations engendered a set of inferences by which the 1977 winter experience could be described and analyzed. The actual case studies identified the following areas of agreement and disagreement with the theoretical propositions:

1. *Operationally,* both school systems factored the crisis of winter 1977 for general education activities.
2. *Symbolically,* and in select specialized activities, neither school system factored their crisis response.
3. The bureaucracies in both systems were limited to marginal adjustment of the normal base of total allocation.
4. Attempts to create a negotiated environment so that the status quo could be retained were undertaken by the Cincinnati local schools, the Cincinnati central office, and the Columbus local schools, but not the Columbus central office.
5. Both systems operated on short-run decision-making during winter 1977 but engaged in a minimum of groupthink or calculated inactivity.
6. Both systems reverted to prewinter 1977 arrangements for schooling as soon as possible after crisis adaptation.

These findings, which concern the actual decision-making of large school systems in winter 1977, will now be considered for their relation to the concepts of rational decision, organizational adaptation, and crisis.

Rationality

The rationality of decision-making is a function of demonstrating consistency between a particular choice and the precedent of past decisions and/or the parameters of a projected future. The 1977 experience suggests that the need for such demonstration varies with the stages or phases of crisis. In the fall of 1976, considerations of how to meet anticipated shortages of natural gas were referred to existing allocations and possible curtailments. Normal school arrangements were the order of the day because there was no precedent to suggest the dramatic effects of severe weather and fuel shortage.

In the throes of crisis "rational" decisions were based upon the certainty that there was no precedent and that the projected future was unknown. Given those conditions, it was equally appropriate to decide to imitate normal operations or to try something radically different. After the 1977 winter, decisions to return to normal were referenced to the exceptional nature of the crisis which occurred. Guarantees of new decision parameters (for example, at least 70 percent of natural gas supplies to be exempt from curtailment) and other crisis issues which demanded attention contributed to the return to normalcy.

A second context for the demonstration of rationality suggest the variation between institutional and person criteria for deciding. In this winter type of crisis neither school system had existing contingency plans or emergency scenarios to guide deciders. However, the early stages of crisis suggest that those who decide are identified by institutional function and bureaucratic role. (For the weather crisis this meant the central-office technical personnel responsible for plant and the superintendent's cabinet.) Decisions were couched in terms of general institutional expectations rather than the particular configurations of a certain issue.

In the throes of crisis, both systems replaced certain institutionally defined deciders with people selected for their individual capacities. For example, in Columbus, the emergency operations center was run by the adult education supervisor. In Cincinnati the host-guest arrangement was supervised by a regional, secondary-school administrator. The rationality which placed certain people in crucial decision roles was the peculiar nature of the winter crisis.

This study suggests that future research into the rationality of decision-making should consider the demonstration of choice as a function of crisis stages and the identification of actual deciders as a function of different points of time.

Adaptive Capacity

The adaptive capacity of a large bureaucracy is purported to be a function of the ability to reallocate base resources and/or of the extent to which uncertainty can be avoided. This case study attempted to describe the extent to which crisis adaptation could be explained by interorganizational and intraorganizational variations of select indicators. The experiences of both Columbus and Cincinnati imply that the actual dynamics of adaptation are much more complex and multifaceted than the popular literature about organizational change might suggest. For the last two decades it has been in vogue to discuss how large bureaucracies "muddle along,"[17] unable to redistribute their base allocations of resources. For example, the delineation of fixed allocations which must meet the constraints of existing personnel contracts, state and federal regulations, and the ongoing implementation of previous planning decisions limits the flexibility of a school system's budget. Many practitioners describe real situations where the total adjustable operating budget for reallocation is less than 5 percent. This type of information has been stretched to many decision situations, and in the process has become overgeneralized.

This study advances the idea that a marginal adjustment for adaptation to unusual conditions depends upon (a) what is judged to be the base allocation *during the time of adaptive effort* and (b) whether the description is based upon the total bureaucracy or the composition of subunits which make up the organization. The base allocation for Cincinnati remained relatively stable prior to, during, and after winter 1977. The dynamics of weather conditions, in and of themselves, did not generate new resources or configurations for the school system's base allocation. Consideration of the extent of adaptation taken by Cincinnati could follow the conventional format of calculating costs and redistributing resources from the normal base. This analysis concludes that even the crisis adjustments for pupil transportation, closing certain schools, and practicing extreme conservation during the night time were marginal in relation to the total base of resources by which adaptation decisions could have been made. Alterations for the months of January and February may have exceeded the normal percent of change used to indicate marginal reallocation (up to 5 percent); but, in the context of considering the organization over the 1976-77 school year, the abnormal variations disappear.

Cincinnati officials could have demonstrated (although the teacher strike may have made it impossible or unwise) that the impact of winter 1977 was minimal when the big picture of the school year was considered.

The Columbus experience vividly demonstrates how conclusions about "marginal adjustments" and "muddling" depend upon the time perspective. The meaning of the Columbus base allocation was very different in October 1976, February 1977, and late May 1977. In October reallocation of resources would be judged against normal conditions (that is, state aid, existing contracts). During School Without Schools one could calculate change allocations from the normal (and show much change) or recompute the school systems base for the month of February by adding in the extra resources gained from local, state, and federal sources. Since most emergency practices or innovative changes were financed by extra dollars or free services, the previous normal base would be only marginally adjusted. The same phenomenon occurred in May 1977 when the school system received more compensation for eighteen school days. This again raises the questions of what bureaucratic base allocation a researcher is to judge and whether marginal or significant change has resulted.

A second issue of perspective concerns whether adaptive capacity is based upon the aggregate of the organization as a single unit or the school system con-

sidered as subunits. Columbus and Cincinnati exhibited variations in the type
and extent of change which occurred within specialized services. In Cincinnati
local schools were affected differently by winter 1977, and the extent of change
required depended upon the particular characteristics of a given facility (that is,
type of fuel, number of pupils transported). These findings contravene generalized conclusions about the marginal adjustments of an aggregate system. While
the aggregate statistic may be "true," this information tells very little about specific variations in crisis response which occurred in winter 1977. The aggregate
conclusion tells us even less about the meaning of "adaptive capacity" in the
bureaucracy.[18]

In summary, the meaning of bureaucratic capacity to reallocate resources in
an emergency depends upon the perspective of base allocation. Normal base calculations tend to underestimate internal variations and to present a constrained
picture of actual adaptive capacity.

Crisis

The final question which this study addresses in regard to its theoretical implications concerns the way in which "crisis" is recognized in decision situations.
Two opposing points of view dominate the literature. An evolutionary perspective of crisis recognition is presented as "a gradual growth of doubt . . . arising
from the componding of uncertainty in the minds of actors . . . about the ade-
quacy of cause and effect links from past experiences, about the proper ranking
of values, about the future. . . ."[19] This perspective of a gradual growth of doubt
is contrasted with a second view of crisis recognition which comes as a result of
a "sharp, disjointed series of breakthroughs and transformations . . . where the
problem is not a matter of uncertainty . . . but the certainty that current knowledge will misstate tomorrow's conditions. . . ."[20]

Again, the Columbus and Cincinnati experiences intimate that judgment
about "crisis recognition" is a matter of perspective. For example, the decision
situation for officials in both systems during mid-January 1977 reflected both
the "gradual growth" of doubt and the certainty that "today's" knowledge
would misstate "tomorrow's" situations. This dual perspective dominated January decisions about pupil transportation, securing self-help gas, and other major
choices. Its impact on deciders was the recognition that (a) this was a crisis,
(b) that the situation was "irrational," and (c) that some type of action had to
be taken.[21]

After the unusual winter conditions eased, the meaning of crisis and essence
of how the schools had decided in such a situation also depended upon perspective. The radical adjustments of Columbus were referenced to the "sharp transformations" of winter 1977. At the same time (under the same weather conditions), Cincinnati officials had difficulty concerning state officials of why they
should receive emergency compensation. Part of their trouble was due to the

projected image that the conditions of January and February had only created gradual doubts" which had been quickly eliminated.

Speculations upon Future Research

The theoretical consideration of what constitutes rational decision-making, organizational capacity for adaptation, and recognition of crisis conditions unveils several important needs for future policy research about the impact of unusual weather on school systems.

First, issues of rationality raise questions about the meaning of planning under crisis conditions.

Table 10-1 identifies four styles of planning based upon distributions of power, predomininant forms of control, methods of implementation, and characteristic roles of the technical experts.

This effort showed that style seems to depend upon the time phase of the crisis period, upon whether the description emphasized symbolic or operational indicators, and upon whether information was gathered from central-office or local-school participants. Each finding forms a basis for research hypotheses in future study.

Second, issues of adaptive capacity suggest the need for future longitudinal study about the relation of type and degree of organizational modification over time. Figure 10-1 illustrates Lowi's distinction between cyclical and structural change which affects the "stability" of a decision system.

Table 10-1
Typology of Crisis Planning

Variables	Command Planning	Policies Planning	Corporate Planning	Participant Planning
Distribution of power	Strongly centralized	Weakly centralized	Fragmented	Dispersed
Form of control	Sanctions	Restructuring of the decision environment	Normative compliance	Voluntary compliance
Method of implementation	Compulsory targets	Mixed field controls general rules inducements	Bargaining (few negotiators: corporate structure)	Participating in decision processes (many participants: community structure)
Role of expert	Bureaucratic specialist	Advisor	Negotiator and broker	Organizer and advocate

Source: Reprinted with kind permission from John Friedmann, *Retracking America: A Theory of Transactive Planning* (Garden City, N.Y.: Doubleday, 1973), p. 71.

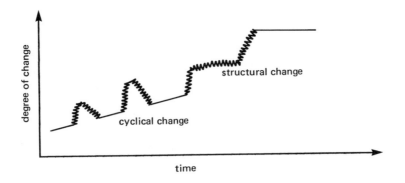

Source: reprinted with kind permission from Theodore Lowi, *At the Pleasure of the Mayor* (New York: Free Press, 1964), p. 191.
Figure 10-1. Models of Stability Over Time

Although this study lacked the methodological characteristics of an extended longitudinal analysis, there was some indication of different patterns of response over time. Future research could explore the fundamental question of whether the organizational changes attributed to weather conditons form a cyclical pattern of adaptation.

Finally, the issue of crisis recognition raises research questions about the meaning of deciding in school organizations when faced with conditions of extreme uncertainty. If the deciison situation is truly unprecedented or novel for some period of time (that is, several weeks or a month), what is the impact upon the bureaucracy? Ernest Haas[22] has studied the European Common Market since 1968 and speculates upon just such a condition. He theorizes that the "turbulence"[23] of uncertainty has created a form of organization and decision-making process called "fragmented issue linkage." Haas notes that

> this style does not occur until sharp dissatisfaction with earlier incrementalist procedures is manifest . . . until the knowledge and experience which had fueled incremental processes are subjected to sharp doubts . . . fragmented issue linkage *tends to characterize the newer issue areas* where classification by conventional, institutional terms are missing.[24]

The actual dynamics of fragmented issue linkage seen to exhibit no automatic shared objectives of decision-makers, either in terms of outcomes or passionate commitment for new organization. There is a deliberate search for new knowledge of crisis decision-making and an overt skepticism toward incremental "solutions." Actual decision processes are often logrolling, package deals which might relate the new issue to other seemingly unrelated issues but without the creation of new common institutions. Finally, system-wide consideration is usually limited to problem recognition, with actual decision activities decentralized.[25]

The characteristics of social organization under crisis conditions of fragmented issue linkage are labeled "asymmetrical overlap."[26] Such an organization has a determined arena, with no clear-cut division of competencies, no single source of authority; several units of power are each primarily responsible for some item within the package of linkages which surrounds an issue. Most important, "the pattern of organization, unlike a formal constitution, is not permanent; the flow of information and authority will be rearranged as new knowledge and learning patterns are incorporated. . . ."[27]

Except for the fact that this new theory of crisis adaptation directly offends conventional sensibilities, could not this interpretation have real meaning for the study of school systems facing crisis? In 1977, neither Columbus nor Cincinnati schools had a "sufficient degree of doubt" about assumptions of incrementalism to consider this interpretation. However, winter 1977 did demonstrate the issue of energy as a new form of scarcity. As the 1980s progress and growing resource scarcities force increasing scrutiny of existing decision arrangements, the hypotheses of Ernest Haas seem a fertile ground for research about complex school organizations in crisis.

Notes

1. Max Weber, *The Theory of Social and Economic Organization*, translated by A.M. Henderson and T. Parsons (New York: Free Press, 1947).

2. It is beyond the scope of this effort to present a full description of bureaucracy. Readers unfamiliar with the literature in this area might consider the following references: Robert Presthus, *The Organizational Society* (New York: Knopf, 1962); Anthony Downs, *Inside Bureaucracy* (Boston: Little, Brown, 1957); R. Cyert and J. March, *The Behavioral Theory of the Firm* (Englewood Cliffs: Prentice-Hall, 1963); and Graham Allisons's discussion of Model II in *Essence of Decision* (Boston: Little, Brown, 1971).

3. Yehezkel Dror, *Public Policymaking Re-Examined* (San Francisco: Chandler, 1966), p. 132.

4. Again, detailed discussion is beyond the scope of this text. The reader interested in an overview of variations in decision-making and some questions about the classic assumptions might consider the following sources: Dror (especially pp. 134-149); Herbert Simon, "The Architecture of Complexity," in the *Science of the Artificial* (Cambridge: MIT Press, 1968), pp. 84-118; Allison, discussion of Model III; Charles Lindblom, "The Science of Muddling Through," *Public Administration Review* 19 (1959), 79-88; and Aaron Wildavsky, "Doing

Better and Feeling Worse: The Political Pathology of Health Policy," *Daedalus*, Winter 1977, pp. 105-123.

5. The author's bias should be declared in relation to the controversy of interpretation which surrounds the description of social organization. Although this effort relies on the behavioralist "what is" interpretation, there is another interpretation often called "social modeling." For an excellent discussion of this controversy, see Chris Argyris, "Some Limits to Rational Man Organizational Theory," *Public Administration Review*, May/June 1974, pp. 253-267.

6. "Bounded" is a term coined by Herbert Simon in *Models of Man* (New York: Wiley, 1957). On page three of his text, Simon declared that "classic" rationality required the "powers of prescience and capacities for computation resembling those we usually attribute to God." See, especially, pp. 204-263.

7. For detailed discussion of some of the theoretical implications of these realities the reader may wish to consult these sources:

a. Concerning the extent that rate of change is affected by size, differentiation, and interdependence of bureaucratic components, see John Ruggie, "Complexity, Planning and Public Order," in Todd LaPorte, eds., *Organized Social Complexity* (Princeton: Princeton University Press, 1975), pp. 119-148: and Robert Keohane and Joseph Nye, "Interdependence and Integration," in F. Greenstein and N. Polsby, eds., *Handbook of Political Science*, (Andover: Addison-Wesley, 1975).

b. Concerning the costs and benefits of organizational maintenance and status quo, see Martin Landau, "Redundancy, Rationality and the Problem of Duplicaton and Overlap," *Public Administration Review* 29 (1969), 246-258: and Donald Schon, *Beyond the Stable State* (New York: Random House, 1971). For a much more techical discussion, see Morris Friedell, "Organizations as Semilattices," *American Sociological Review* 27 (1967), 46-54.

c. Concerning the comparison of cybernetic, analytic probability, and cognitive categorization perspectives about choice, see John Steinbruner, *The Cybernetic Theory of Decision* (Princeton: Princeton University Press, 1974).

d. Concerning an extended discussion about bureaucracies in the public sector, see Victor Fuchs, "The First Service Economy," *Public Interest*, Winter 1966, pp. 1-17.

8. See Allison. Also, consult Alexander George, "Adaptation to Stress in Political Decision Making," in A. George, G. Coelho, and others, eds., *Coping*

and Adaptation (New York: Basic Books, 1974) pp. 175-234; and Irving Janis, "Groupthink among Policy Makers," in N. Sanford and C. Cornstock, eds., *Sanctions for Evil* (San Francisco: Jossey-Bass, 1971) and "Group Identification under Conditions of External Danger," *British Journal of Medical Psychology* 26 (1963), 230-242.

9. Allison, p. 84. Reprinted with permission. This same argument is presented in an economic context as the "mature" organization whose basic motivation is not to maximize profits *per se* but to minimize risks during the gestation period between decision and product by controlling the social environment. See John Galbraith, *Economics and Public Purpose* (Boston: Houghton Mifflin, 1973). From this economic perspective, the "external environment" includes price, consumer demand, source of supply, and government.

10. Allison, p. 171.

11. Janis, "Groupthink."

12. Janis, "Group Identification," p. 234.

13. Much work has been done in the area of mathematical gaming, particularly on the two phenomena of "extrarational" choice called the "Prisoner's Dilemma" and the "Chicken Game." See Dror, p. 151; Anatol Rapoport and J. Chammah, *Prisoner's Dilemma* (Ann Arbor: University of Michigan Press, 1965); Allen Liske, *The Consistency Controversy* (New York, Wiley, 1975); and N. Howard, *Paradoxes of Rationality* (Cambridge: MIT Press, 1971).

14. Cited in George, p. 224.

15. Again, field discussion is limited by the intent of this effort. The reader may wish to consult the following sources for more information: David Easton, *A Systems Analysis of Political Life* (New York: Wiley, 1965); Walter Buckley, "Society as an Adaptive System," in W. Buckley, ed., *Modern Systems Research for the Behavioral Sciences* (Chicago: Aldine, 1968); and Robert Chin, "The Utility System Models and Developmental Models for Practitioners," in W. Bennis, K. Benne, and R. Chin, *The Planning of Change*, 2nd edition (New York: Holt, Rinehart, and Winston, 1969), pp. 297-312.

16. For a documentation of the failure of conventional planning assumptions about dynamic change in noncrisis conditions, see Paul Berman and Milbrey McLaughlin, *Federal Programs Supporting Educational Change*, Volumes 1-5 (Santa Monica: Rand Corporation, R-1589, April 1975).

17. Lindblom.

18. This finding is also similar to interpretations of planned change as "partisan mutual adjustments" among key individuals rather than formal, structural modifications. See Berman and McLauglin.

19. Ernest Haas, "Turbulent Fields and the Theory of Regional Integration," *International Organization* 3:2 (Spring 1976), 184. Reprinted with permission.

20. John Friedmann, and Barclay Hudson, "Knowledge and Action: Guide to Planning Theory," *Journal of American Institute of Planning*, January 1974, p.14.

21. This is consistent with hints to cope with uncertainty by taking immediate action to help block the "infinite regress of important, unanswered questions. . . ." Dale Mann, *Policy Decision Making in Education* (New York: Teachers College Press, 1975), pp. 139-144.

22. Haas, pp. 173-212.

23. An attempt to state the formal properties of turbulence is found in J.L. Metcalfe, "Systems Models, Economic Models and the Causal Texture of Organizational Environments," *Human Relations* 27 (1974), 836-863.

24. Haas, pp. 184-206. Haas specifically notes *energy* as a new issue.

25. Ibid., pp. 190-191.

26. Ibid., p. 206.

27. Ibid., pp. 207-208. A second level of this idea might be to distinguish between technological uncertainties and strategic uncertainties. See Albert Madansky, "Uncertainty," in E.S. Quade and W. Boucher, eds., *Systems Analysis and Policy Planning* (New York: Elsevier, 1968), pp. 81-97.

Appendix A
Chronology

The following are selected events which contributed to the circumstances of winter 1977.

1972-1974: The public utility which serves the Columbus schools filed the initial curtailment plan with the state regulatory commission (July 24, 1972); Cincinnati schools have the base allocation for twenty large natural gas user buildings calculated on the twelve-month usage in 1972; Columbus schools organize the first Energy Crisis Committee (October 1973); the State Department of Education names an energy coordinator for Ohio schools (October 1973) and issues guidelines for closing schools due to lack of fuel (January 1974); Columbus schools have their base allocation calculated on the highest twelve-month use of all natural gas user schools between 1972 and 1974; State Board of Education adopts resolution supporting energy as an educational concern (November 11, 1974).

Winter, Spring 1975: Columbia Gas of Ohio asks for certain domestic customers to be exempt from natural gas curtailments in an emergency but does not include public schools (January 10); the state regulatory commission (P.U.C.O.) approves the heating season curtailment plan for 40 percent of the large user Columbus school base allocations during winter months and 15 percent curtailment during other months (January 16); Cincinnati schools told by the gas transmission company that their large user schools could be curtailed 28 percent during the 1975-76 winter (April 30); the Cincinnati utility applies for a curtailment plan (June 20).

Summer, Fall 1975: The carryover of surplus gas between seasons of allocation is eliminated for Columbus schools (July 29); Columbus schools notified of a 40 percent large user curtailment during the 1975 winter (August 25); Cincinnati schools told to expect 20 percent large user curtailment *if* there is an emergency (September 11); State Department of Education holds a series of energy workshops for local schools (August, September, December); Columbus completes first internal fuel consumption analysis (October 23); 40 percent large user curtailment plan implemented for Columbus schools (November 3).

Winter, Spring 1976: Guidelines to secure self-help gas distributed by state regulatory commission (March 30); SDE distributes energy materials for teachers in all Ohio schools; state regulatory commission approves plan for 100 percent curtailment of large commercial users.

Summer, Fall 1976: Columbus officials refuse to purchase surplus gas (September 14); Columbus schools notified of 40 percent large user curtailment for 1977 winter (October 14); gas transmission company mandated to carry emergency fuel by Federal Power Commission (December 14); Cincinnati schools told that large user facilities would be curtailed 20 percent (December 30).

Cincinnati: Winter 1977

January 3-7: All schools closed for inclement weather (5); no pupil transportation (6,7). By Friday 7, average temperature 14° with seven inches of snow on ground.

January 10-14: All schools closed (10); no pupil transportation (11, 12, 13, 14). By Friday 14, average temperature 30° with seven inches of snow on ground.

January 17-21: A holiday (17); no pupil transportation (18); schools closed as calendar days (19, 20, 21); average temperature on Friday 20° with nine inches of snow.

January 22: Governor declares state-wide emergency.

January 24-28: No pupil transportation (24,25); utility curtails Cincinnati schools 30 percent (27); the utility mandates all schools to curtail natural gas 80 percent and all Cincinnati schools close (28). Average temperature 12°, with twelve inches of snow by Friday (28).

January 29-30: Impact of crisis becomes overt; officials consider three day per week plan. Average temperature is 2° with twelve inches of snow on Saturday.

January 31, February 2-4: All schools closed (31); large natural gas schools closed (1, 2); public utility curtails all large user schools 30 percent (1); Board of Education holds open meeting to discuss crisis (1); legislature passes "emergency day" relief legislation (2); thermostats in all gas schools set at 60° for operation, 35-40° for nighttime (3); host-guest pairing of local schools begins (3); Cincinnati officials find pupils transported as guests not getting lunches (4); average temperature on Friday (4) 31° with four inches of snow on ground.

February 5: State Department of Education issues statement asking public schools to be exempt from gas curtailments.

February 7-11: Bus tokens issued to guest students (8); gas to area parochial schools curtailed 80 percent. Schools declare they will shut down until April 1 or until curtailment lifted (9). Friday (11) average temperature 49° with one inch of snow on ground.

February 14-18: Schools provide box lunches to guest students riding buses (16); SDE states it will not pay transportation compensation (18). Average temperature on Friday (18) 36° with a trace of snow remaining.

February 21-25: All schools closed for holiday (21); desegregationists argue emergency busing for energy demonstrates the feasibility of doing same to achieve racial balance (21). Average temperature by Friday (25) 48° with no snow remaining.

February 28, March 4: School canceled for guest students (1); all schools return to normal arrangements and thermostats raised to 65°(2); bus token plan discontinued (3); by Friday (4) average temperature 41° with one inch of snow on the ground.

Columbus: Winter 1977

January 3-7: School holiday (3); all large user schools curtailed to 50 percent and Energy Committee meets in emergency session (2); Board of Education questions administrators about plight (7). Average temperature on Friday (7) 13° with 5 inches of snow on ground.

January 10-14: Other natural gas schools (small users) curtailed 10 percent (10); self-help gas committee meets for first time (10); all schools closed (10, 11) because of hazardous weather; average temperature on Friday (14) 27° with seven inches of snow on ground.

January 17-21: All schools closed for holiday (17); all schools closed for hazardous weather (18); central office begins planning of School Without Schools and starts the *Handbook* (20). Average temperature on Friday (21) 17° with nine inches of snow on ground.

January 22: Governor declares state-wide natural gas emergency.

January 24-28: Large user schools curtailed to 85 percent (24); state regulatory commission sets emergency cost arrangement for securing self-help gas (26); all schools closed due to energy emergency (28). On Friday (28) average temperature 10° with eleven inches of snow on ground.

January 31, February 1-4: Schools closed for energy emergency (31, 1); School Without Schools plan approved (31); meeting of all local school administrators to explain cluster arrangements and to issue *Handbook* (1); legislature passes emergency relief legislation (2); first self-help gas well hooked to pipeline (4). Temperature on February 4 averages 28° with nine inches of snow on ground.

February 7-11: All normal schooling replaced with School Without Schools arrangement (7, 8, 9, 10, 11); first self-help gas reaches Columbus school meter (9). Average temperature on Friday (11) 40° with a trace of snow.

February 14-18: All normal schooling replaced with School Without Schools (14, 15, 16, 17, 18); legislature passes bill which allows schools to receive compensation for field trips taken because of emergency (17); state regulatory commission announces curtailment to be modified due to federal legislation. Average temperature on Friday (18) 25° with one inch of snow on ground.

February 21-25: All normal schooling replaced with School Without Schools (21, 22, 23, 24, 25). Gas curtailments raised to 50 percent of base allocation (22). Average temperature on Friday (25) 46° with no snow on ground.

February 28, March 1-4: All schools closed for "early" spring break (28, 1, 2, 3, 4); gas curtailments raised to 40 percent (28). Average temperature on Friday (4) 30° with no snow on ground.

Appendix B
Case Study
Methodology

The information and findings reported in the study were the result of an exhaustive case analysis which was conducted in terms of the appropriate methodology for field research.[1] The major purpose was to describe crisis response by the identification of variations in decision-making within and between the two school systems under study. Six foci (called major variables) were assumed to contribute to generalizations about interorganizational and intraorganizational variations in decision-making. This could, in turn, be used to infer crisis response of Columbus and Cincinnati schools during winter 1977. While the description is important, what can we say about the applicability of lessons learned to other school systems? What can be said about the appropriate direction for methodological "building" on this effort? To the extent this study is used *as a guide* to help in the selection, description, and analysis of an unusual decision condition, it has value in (a) the detailed presentation of the data and (b) the open declaration that generalizations about what occurred in Cincinnati and Columbus in 1977 have no assumption of an empirically derived foundation. The value of a case study is like a metaphor rather than a stringent guide for the replication, control, and prediction criteria of scientific inquiry.[2] A conscious decision was made to limit the methodological assumptions concerning the "explanatory relationship" of the six major variables to the "dependent" variables of interorganizational and intraorganizational variations in decision response. The limitation was made because of the methodological issues of interaction and dimensionality which are inherent in describing the crisis type of phenomena. Interaction and dimensionality are, in the case of the novel situation, true issues of accurate description. They are not even part of the normal arguments of determinants research[3] about the statistical complexities which confound a researcher's ability either to make precise statements or to generalize about the effect of specific variables on decision response. In the final analysis, this study stopped short of trying to find "causality" because the development of a conceptually tractable, general model of school system crisis response seems premature at this time. Hopefully, this is not perceived as an apology for a poor effort, but a methodological call for more reality and less pretension in policy research dealing with the crisis phenomena. The true issue is the legitimacy of doing more than exploration when crisis has to recognize that statistical error may outweigh systematic variation and that the theoretical dimension of certain variables lacks the characteristic of direct observation.[4]

The Dilemma

The Downs[5] study of how bureaucratic innovativeness relates to a number of socioeconomic, task, environment, bureaucratic, and executive characteristic variables demonstrates the dilemma. Stringent adherence to determinants research methodology made the Downs effort a "tight" study in relation to what is often assumed to be legitimate policy research. Yet the substantive results of the study were meager *if considered with any expectation other than to accomplish nominal description and engaging a hypothesis "generating" effort.*[6] Serious students of policy research should be concerned with such findings as:

> ... the evidence suggests that the only dimension of the socioeconomic environment that is a significant determinant of [bureaucratic] innovation is something we have labeled socioeconomic heterogeneity ... a dimension composed to various indicators of social and economic "cleavages."[7]

or

> ... the provisional hypothesis that the ability of the bureaucracy to independently determine policy (i.e., its decomposability from its environment) is not constant but is contingent on the degree of uncertainty which surrounds a policy area.[8]

The lack of definitive substantive outcomes occurs when one tries to over-extend methodological reality. Without a doubt, this study of school system response to winter crisis would have been caught in the same dilemma which Downs identifies as problems of interaction and dimensionality. In describing interaction, the following caution is given:

> ... if complex interaction is as common as there is reason to suspect, the development of ... models may be almost impossible. Suppose, for instance, that the impact of organizational complexity depends upon five, six or even more factors ... while in theory such fifth and sixth order interaction effects can be discovered and handled statistically, the *incorporation of several variables whose impact is so unstable in any model makes great demands on sample size, greatly violates the norm of parsimony and, as a practical matter, makes parameter estimation unfeasible.* (emphasis added)[9]

Certainly the six major variables of this study could raise the interaction issue. The lesson of overextension is applicable to the whole methodological context of empirical attempts. The real conclusions may be that the impact of many variables in complex interaction is effectively idiosyncratic to the choice situation and that any arrived-at variable coefficient can be expected to vary dramatically depending on the context of the decision.[10] If that is the nature of the policy phenomenon, then systematic study of crisis must address reality situation by situation.

The second major methodological concern, dimensionality, goes even further to challenge the descriptive meanings of the six major variables from an empirical standpoint. The issue concerns whether a particular variable or indicator of a variable is an "observable."[11] Observables are "immediately susceptible to direct sensory observation and hence are often called descriptive terms."[12] The six major variables of this study are "theoretical concepts" because they are abstractions only indicated by observables, not the observable characteristics themselves. Until the day of universal agreement about the relation of observables to abstract construction, the dimensionality issue will continue to plague the selection and description of "policy variables" in determinant research. The present state of the art mandates only a logic of "if . . . then" to link observation to abstraction. We are a far cry from empirical verification in the study of stress, novel decision-making, and response patterns of large, complex organizations.

Suggestions for Future Research

Given the above arguments, it seems advisable that policy research continue the descriptive, "grounded theory" approach to the study of crisis decision response. Because we know the distinction between reality and statistical assumption, there should be more of the creative application of methodology which may ignore some of the basic assumptions which specify conventional legitimacies. This is not a call for ignorant or sloppy researchers, rather researchers who emphasize substance over methodological form (or at least recognize when methodological form is, in and of itself, the substance). From this perspective, the "proportion of accounted for variance" may be less important than the basic fact that, in a particular factor analysis, the first rotation identified a certain cluster arrangement before the second (or sixth or ninth) rotation identified another clustering. Numerical "values" may only be place markers of gross ordering rather than symbols of ordinal assumptions. Of course, we prostitute the power of the statistic, but when we are dealing with apples and oranges or clouds and clocks what is wrong with a "primitive" interpretation? These data suggest that nominal description and hypothesis-generating activities are important objectives and the present context for research designed to understanding the winter crisis.

Notes

1. For example, W. Richard Scott, "Field Methods in the Study of Organizations," in *Handbook of Organizations*; and Richard Adams and Jack Preiss, eds., *Human Organization Research* (Homewood, Ill.: Dorsey Press, 1960).
2. For an extended discussion see James Price, "Design of Proof in Organizational Research," and William Starbuck, "Some Comments, Observations and Objections Stimulated by 'Design of Proof,' " *Administrative Science Quarterly* 13 (June 1968), 121-134, 134-161.

3. Also called comparative policy research, rationalized as the principal vehicle to guide the developement of a "positive theory" of public policy formation. See, for example, Thomas R. Dye, *Politics, Economics, and the Public* (Chicago: Rand McNally, 1966); Brian Fry and Richard Winters, "The Politics of Redistribution," *American Political Science Review* 64 (1970), 508-522.

4. Or when direct observation negates popular theory and the discipline is in pursuit of a new theory to rationalize existing contradiction. See also Paul Feyerabend, *Against Method* (London: NLB, 1976).

5. George Downs, Jr., *Bureaucracy, Innovation and Public Policy* (Lexington, Mass.: Lexington Books, D.C. Heath and Company, Copyright 1976, D.C. Heath and Company). Reprinted with permission.

6. See Barney Glaser and Anselim Strauss, *The Discovery of Grounded Theory* (Chicago: Aldine, 1967).

7. Downs, p. 115.

8. Ibid., p. 126.

9. Ibid., p. 128.

10. See Ernest Haas, "Turbulent Fields and the Theory of Regional Integration," *International Organization* 30:2 (1976), 173-212.

11. David Willer and Murray Webster, "Theoretical Concepts and Observables," *American Sociological Review* 35 (1970, pl.), 748-757.

12. Ibid., p. 749.

Index

Absenteeism. *See* Pupil attendance

"Adaptive capacity," of large bureaucracy, 131, 137-139. *See also* Decision-making

Administrators: of Columbus and Cincinnati schools, 52, 53, 54; effect of emergency arrangements on responsibilities of, 63-64. *See also* Central office arrangements

AFL-CIO, 21

Aiken senior high school: effects of crisis arrangement on, 75; normal characteristics of, 70, 71, 73

Allison, Graham, 134

Alpine elementary school: effects of crisis arrangement on, 77, 78, 110-111, 113; normal characteristics of, 69, 71, 72

Alternative fuel, conversion to, 83-84, 86, 95

Athletic programs, during School Without Schools plan, 58, 77, 99

Attendance. *See* Pupil attendance

Autonomy, of local schools during crisis, 99-103; in Cincinnati, 103-108; in Columbus, 108-113

Avondale elementary school: effects of crisis arrangement on, 75, 104-106; normal characteristics of, 70, 71, 73

Base allocation, of gas supplies, 9-11; and adaptive capacities of bureaucracies, 137-139; and "carryover" natural gas, 84-85; seasonal system of, 10, 11, 31, 84-85; and use of "creative accounting" plan, 32, 84; user classifications for determining, 21, 30, 34, 83; utilities' calculations of, 30-31, 32. *See also* Natural gas fuel

Boards of education: of Cincinnati and Columbus compared, 46-47, 49;

role of, in long-range energy planning, 120. *See also* Community relationships

Brookhaven senior high school: effects of crisis arrangement on, 77, 78, 112; normal characteristics of, 69, 70, 71, 72

Burdett elementary school: effects of crisis on, 74; normal characteristics of, 70, 71, 73

"Calculated inactivity," defined, 134, 135. *See also* Decision-making

"Carryover" natural gas, 84-85, 95. *See also* Natural gas fuel

Case study: procedure for, 2-5; purpose of, 5-6

Central office arrangements: in case study analysis, 3, 4; in Cincinnati school system, 52, 53, 59-63, 75, 105-106; in Columbus school system, 52, 54-59, 109; and role in short- and long-range energy planning, 120, 121. *See also* Local school arrangements

Chicago elementary school: effects of crisis arrangement on, 77, 78; normal characteristics of, 69, 70, 71, 72

Cincinnati Federation of Teachers, 88. *See also* Teachers

Cincinnati Gas and Electric (CG and E), 9; base allocation calculations of, 30-31; gas curtailment procedures of, 13, 16, 31, 33; relationship of, with supplier, 29, 33

Cincinnati Superintendent of Schools, responsibilities of, during winter emergency, 60, 61. *See also* Central office arrangements

Cluster centers: for school desegregation, 22; in School Without Schools plan, 76, 79, 87, 99, 109

About the Author

David K. Wiles has combined scholarship and research in the study of school politics, particularly two-tiered governance and energy-related issues. He is a professor of educational administration at the State University of New York at Albany and has previously served on the faculty at Miami University, Virginia Polytechnic Institute, and the University of Toronto. Professor Wiles' writings include *Changing Perspectives of Educational Research* (1972), *Political Interpretations of Educational Administration* (1976), and (with coauthors) *Practical Politics for School Administrators* (1979).